D0406801

The
SUPER EASY
BABY FOOD
Cookbook

THE

SUPER EASY BABY FOOD

COOKBOOK

HEALTHY HOMEMADE RECIPES
FOR EVERY AGE & STAGE

Anjali Shah

Photography by Leslie Grow

ROCKRIDGE
PRESS

Copyright © 2018 by Anjali Shah

No part of this publication may be reproduced, stored in a retrieval system, or transmitted in any form or by any means, electronic, mechanical, photocopying, recording, scanning, or otherwise, except as permitted under Section 107 or 108 of the 1976 United States Copyright Act, without the prior written permission of the publisher. Requests to the publisher for permission should be addressed to the Permissions Department, Rockridge Press, 6005 Shellmound Street, Suite 175, Emeryville, CA 94608.

Limit of Liability/Disclaimer of Warranty: The publisher and the author make no representations or warranties with respect to the accuracy or completeness of the contents of this work and specifically disclaim all warranties, including without limitation warranties of fitness for a particular purpose. No warranty may be created or extended by sales or promotional materials. The advice and strategies contained herein may not be suitable for every situation. This work is sold with the understanding that the publisher is not engaged in rendering medical, legal, or other professional advice or services. If professional assistance is required, the services of a competent professional person should be sought. Neither the publisher nor the author shall be liable for damages arising herefrom. The fact that an individual, organization, or website is referred to in this work as a citation and/or potential source of further information does not mean that the author or the publisher endorses the information the individual, organization, or website may provide or recommendations they/it may make. Further, readers should be aware that websites listed in this work may have changed or disappeared between when this work was written and when it is read.

For general information on our other products and services or to obtain technical support, please contact our Customer Care Department within the United States at (866) 744-2665, or outside the United States at (510) 253-0500.

Rockridge Press publishes its books in a variety of electronic and print formats. Some content that appears in print may not be available in electronic books, and vice versa.

TRADEMARKS: Rockridge Press and the Rockridge Press logo are trademarks or registered trademarks of Callisto Media Inc. and/or its affiliates, in the United States and other countries, and may not be used without written permission. All other trademarks are the property of their respective owners. Rockridge Press is not associated with any product or vendor mentioned in this book.

Design by Lisa Bieser

Photographs © Leslie Grow, 2018
Styling by Jeanette Moncada

Author photo © Nicholas Gang

ISBN: Print 978-1-93975-477-6 | eBook 978-1-93975-478-3

TO MY TWO BEAUTIFUL,
FUNNY, INTERESTING,
FOODIE KIDS WHO
INSPIRED ALL OF THE
RECIPES IN THIS BOOK.

TO MY HUSBAND AND
BEST FRIEND WHO HAS
SUPPORTED ME EVERY
STEP OF THE WAY.

CONTENTS

INTRODUCTION

Even before my daughter, Layla, was born, I had ideas about the type of eater I wanted her to be. I hoped she'd be as passionate about food as I am and excited to try a variety of foods. As a new mom, I was determined to make all of my kids' baby food at home from scratch. Being a trained nutritionist, I knew it was the healthier choice. Homemade baby food packs a bigger nutritional punch than store-bought versions and is less processed since you don't need to add any preservatives to homemade purées. Additionally, most store-bought purées are fruit forward. This means that even though *spinach* might be featured on the label, it's usually one of the last ingredients (after apple or pear purée). By making my own baby food, I knew I'd be able to control the ingredients and introduce my kids to a variety of flavors and spices early to develop their palates. In addition to these benefits, it's much more cost-effective to make baby food at home.

In short, it was a win-win-win plan—in theory, at least. In truth, I was a little worried about how I was going to incorporate preparing healthy baby food into my already busy life. In those exhausting early days of parenthood, could I realistically dedicate my already limited time and energy to cooking healthy and delicious meals for my little girl? I decided I had to try. At first, I remember looking for recipes that were both simple and flavorful, but I couldn't find a reliable one-stop resource with recipes that would take me all the way from infancy to toddlerhood. So I set about creating my own recipes based on my knowledge of nutrition and appealing flavor combinations. Soon, my clients, friends, and family members were asking me what foods to give their babies. Everyone seemed to have the same concerns as I did: *What foods are the most nutritious for my little one? How can I make sure that I don't end up with a picky eater?* And most frequently: *I want to make baby food at home, but how can I fit it in my busy schedule as a working parent?*

After a bit of trial and error, I created these simple and delicious recipes that I'm excited to share with you, so you can do this, too. Feeding your precious baby nutritious and wholesome foods in an easy, streamlined way is what this book is all about. And I promise, even sleep-deprived new parents can manage these recipes. Almost all of the recipes in this book can be made in bulk ahead of time and in less than 30 minutes. If you can devote even one hour to food prep on weekends, you'll have meals you

can thaw in minutes for the weeks ahead. Once I took the plunge, I was hooked—in fact, it became *easier* to whip up a quick purée with ingredients I had on hand than to rush out to the store with baby in tow to grab off-the-shelf baby foods I didn't feel great about. For you, once you develop your own system, you'll not only enjoy the convenience of making homemade food but also experience incredible satisfaction from knowing you're feeding your child healthy and delicious meals that you created with love.

I hope you'll look at this book as your guide. It contains recipes tailored for every age from 6 to 36 months and simple methods that will ensure you always have wholesome and flavorful foods on hand. The recipes are organized by age, but you can always mix and match recipes as your little one gets older (for example, you can mix purées from the earlier chapters into some of the chunkier recipes in the later chapters). The early chapters include simple, single-ingredient purées that take mere minutes to prepare; the later chapters feature easy, big-kid meals the whole family can enjoy. In each chapter, I suggest spices and herbs you can add to help develop your baby's palate and build his or her appreciation for all types of food.

I remember being a little daunted when I started making Layla's baby food for the first time. But through a bit of trial and error, I figured it out. And with this book as a guide, it will be even easier for you!

PART ONE

A WHOLESOME BEGINNING

Chapter One

STARTING SOLIDS

Welcome to the wonderful world of solid foods! If you're reading this, your baby has probably shown signs that he or she is ready for solids. You may be wondering, *What food should we try first? Will my baby like it? What food is solid but not too solid? What if my baby spits it out everywhere?* Yes, starting solids is a big and exciting step—as well as a messy one. If you're feeling a little nervous or overwhelmed, don't worry—this is meant to be fun and satisfying. With the right tools and recipes, you'll have baby-food prep mastered in no time. So let's get started.

IS MY BABY READY?

It can be difficult to interpret baby's cues, and pediatricians' recommendations differ regarding when to begin solid foods. Some say that babies are ready at four months, others, at six months, and still others suggest waiting until baby "seems ready." We introduced solids around five months because our daughter was staring at us whenever we ate anything, the drool literally pouring out of her mouth.

You can keep an eye out for these signs that your child might be ready.

- Your baby has good head control.
- Your baby is able to sit well with support (such as in a high chair).
- Your baby shows interest in food by watching you while you eat, drooling while you eat, moving his mouth while you eat, or reaching for your food.
- Your baby exhibits a diminished tongue-thrust reflex (which means he can actually swallow the food versus just pushing it out of his mouth).

If your baby hasn't shown these signs yet, don't worry. He'll show you when he's ready.

BABY'S FIRST SPOONFUL

It's time for that first spoonful of food! But what to offer your little one first? For a long time, pediatricians almost universally recommended rice cereal as baby's first food. However, for the past several years, the American Academy of Pediatrics has recommended introducing a "wide variety of foods," starting with any vegetable or fruit. Giving your baby a wide variety of foods will help develop her palate and ensure her love and appreciation of different flavors for the rest of her life. Have fun with the possibilities! Take a peek at chapter 3 to get some ideas for single-ingredient purées, most of which can be an ideal first food for your baby.

We opted for avocado as Layla's first food because it has a mild flavor, isn't too sweet, has a creamy texture, and is filled with healthy fats, vitamins, and minerals. When it comes time to choose, I recommend avocado, sweet potato, or pear, which are all high in fiber, mild in flavor, not too sweet, and rich in vitamins. If your baby rejects these flavors at first, don't get discouraged. Just keep offering, and eventually your baby will grow to love the foods he or she rejected the first (or tenth) time around.

FOOD REACTIONS

As you start feeding your baby solids, you may be worried about allergic reactions. Food allergies seem to be everywhere these days, so it's certainly a valid concern. When introducing foods, the order in which you do so is less important than making sure you offer new foods carefully and attentively. The best way to detect any adverse reaction is to introduce new foods one at a time, and wait 48 hours after introducing a new food before trying another one. That way, you can be sure your baby has no reaction to it before introducing the next food. It's also ideal to introduce new foods in the morning, so you can watch for signs of any allergic reaction later in the day.

Gagging and Choking

Don't worry if your baby gags a bit when tasting a new food or first learning to eat solids. Eating solids is a completely different "skill" than drinking milk, so the first few times he swallows, it might seem like your baby is gagging or about to spit up. If he seems to reject it, the purée might be too chunky, or the taste of the purée might be too strong.

Choking, however, is different from gagging. This usually happens if the food is too large for your baby's throat. If your baby is coughing or gagging, it means her airway is partially blocked. If that's the case, watch her while you let her continue to cough, since coughing is the most effective way to dislodge a blockage. If your baby seems to be truly choking and cannot breathe (that is, cannot cry or cough), you may need to perform back blows and chest thrusts to dislodge the food. In fact, one of the most valuable things you can do as a new parent is to get certified in obstructed-airway procedures and infant CPR before starting solids. If your baby isn't able to cough up the object, ask someone to call 911 while you continue back blows and chest thrusts.

The best way to avoid any kind of gagging or choking reaction is to make sure your purées are very smooth. The ideal purée in the early days of feeding solids is smooth, watery, and thin, served in tiny spoonfuls. Although some foods, like banana or avocado, may seem smooth enough to just mash up, I recommend puréeing even those when your baby is starting out.

As a new parent, wouldn't you like to know what foods are most likely to cause allergic reactions? Here's a useful list of eight foods that the Food and Drug Administration (FDA) identifies as "The Big 8" major food allergens:

1. Cow's milk
2. Eggs
3. Peanuts
4. Tree nuts (e.g., almonds, cashews, walnuts)
5. Fish (e.g., bass, cod, flounder)
6. Shellfish (e.g., crab, lobster, shrimp)
7. Soy
8. Wheat

But guess what? Introducing these foods is still important! Aside from cow's milk, nut butters, and fish high in mercury (see Foods to Avoid in the First Year, page 8), these foods are still best introduced to your baby before the age of one year, as research now shows that early exposure can help reduce allergy risk later in life. So here's how to do it: As you introduce these foods, offer a small amount first, and if your baby shows no reaction for 48 hours, then you can introduce each food into the rotation, gradually increasing the amount of that food over

ALLERGIC REACTION SIGNS

• • •

Signs of a food allergy may occur a few minutes or hours after your baby's first bite, or even a few days later. These are common allergic reaction signs to watch out for after your baby eats a new food:

- Shrill or hoarse-sounding cry
- Gastrointestinal distress such as gas, discomfort, vomiting, or diarrhea
- Runny nose, congestion, cough, or sneezing
- Difficulty breathing
- Skin irritation, such as rashes or hives
- Facial or tongue swelling

If any of these reactions occurs, discontinue the food immediately and call your pediatrician. Rashes may or may not be related to a food allergy, which is why it's always best to consult your child's doctor if you see any symptoms that could potentially be an allergic reaction. Even if it's a false alarm, a good doctor will appreciate your diligence.

time. If you have a family history of food allergies, that doesn't necessarily mean you should avoid those foods for your baby altogether. Instead, introduce those foods under the guidance of your pediatrician (sometimes even in your pediatrician's office) in small quantities (no more than ½ teaspoon), and look for reactions immediately.

If your baby has an allergic response to a certain food, he may outgrow it as he gets older. New research shows that slow, controlled exposure to allergenic foods can result in a decrease in allergenic response over time (note that this is usually done in a pediatrician's office; do not attempt this on your own at home). There is also a distinction between an allergy and a food intolerance or sensitivity. A true food allergy causes an immune system reaction that affects numerous organs in the body. It can cause a range of symptoms such as swelling, hives, rashes, trouble breathing, and swollen airway. In some cases, an allergic food reaction can be severe or even life-threatening.

Food intolerance or sensitivity is usually less serious and often presents as digestive problems (gas, discomfort, fussiness, constipation or diarrhea, indigestion). Certain foods can cause gas in babies. These foods include cruciferous vegetables (broccoli, cauliflower, kale, and Brussels sprouts, for instance), beans and other legumes, and citrus fruits. Usually by the age of six to eight months, babies' digestive systems have matured to the point that these foods shouldn't cause major problems. However, if you find that your baby is prone to gas, you'll probably choose to serve these foods sparingly so your baby isn't too uncomfortable.

AN ORGANIC START

When I started making baby food for Layla, I chose to go organic for almost all of her purées. Organic ingredients are grown without the use of hormones, antibiotics, GMOs (genetically modified organisms), or synthetic pesticides or fertilizers. When you use organic ingredients, you can guarantee that none of these substances end up in your baby's food. In addition, some research has shown that organic foods are higher in nutrients than their conventional counterparts. As a result, the market for organic foods has exploded, and the once-prohibitive price of organic foods has come down. Going organic is more affordable than ever before, which is great news for you and your baby.

Organic still usually costs more than conventional, though, because organic farmers don't receive the same federal subsidies as conventional farmers. And

FOODS TO AVOID IN THE FIRST YEAR

While there are so many foods that your baby can enjoy in her first year, there are a few foods to avoid until your baby turns one year old.

- **Honey:** Honey can contain *Clostridium botulinum*, which can cause infant botulism, a rare but potentially fatal illness in babies. Their digestive systems are immature, which makes them more susceptible to these bacteria than adults.

- **Cow's milk:** While fine for babies over one year old, cow's milk doesn't contain enough essential fatty acids, iron, or vitamin E to be a good replacement for breast milk or formula. It also contains a good deal of protein, *potassium*, and sodium, which are hard on babies' digestive systems. You can introduce yogurt and cheese as early as six to eight months, however, as the lactose has been broken down by the culturing of yogurt or cheese, which limits or removes the troublesome milk proteins and makes it easier to digest.

- **Fish high in mercury:** Too much mercury can harm a child's developing brain and nervous system, so children should avoid king mackerel, marlin, orange roughy, shark, swordfish, tilefish, and ahi tuna (which includes bigeye tuna and yellowfin tuna).

- **Choking hazards:** These include hot dogs, nuts and seeds, chunks of meat or cheese, whole grapes, popcorn, big chunks of raw vegetables or fruits, nut butter, and raisins.

- **Added sugar and processed food:** As a health coach, I always recommend that my clients avoid added sugars and processed foods. Refined sugar has been linked to all kinds of health problems, including obesity, inflammation, heart disease, and high cholesterol. If your child gets used to unnaturally sweet foods (think sugary cereals, flavored yogurts, juice, etc.) at an early age, she may reject wholesome, balanced foods.

- **Known allergens in your family:** Trigger foods may vary, but allergies can run in families. So if you or your partner has a particular allergy, hold off on that food when starting out with solids until you can introduce it under the guidance of your pediatrician.

since organic farmers don't use pesticides and chemical fertilizers, it takes them longer to grow the same amount of crops, making organic farming more labor-intensive. All of that extra work is built into the cost of organic food. But the great thing is this: Even organic homemade baby food is cheaper than store-bought conventional baby food. For example, at my local market, one organic sweet potato costs about $1.50. That sweet potato will make at least 8 servings of baby food, which translates to $0.19 per serving. In contrast, a 4-ounce jar (2 servings) of sweet potato purée costs about $1.05—or $0.53 per serving!

Here are some additional benefits of organic baby food:

- **No risk of contamination:** Organic baby food decreases your infant's exposure to pesticides, synthetic hormones, antibiotics, and heavy metals.
- **Supports sustainable farming:** Organic farming practices reduce pollution, conserve water, reduce soil erosion, increase soil fertility, and use less energy. Farming without pesticides is also better for the local animal population as well as the people who live close to farms.
- **More healthy fats:** Studies have shown that organic meat and dairy can contain about 50 percent more heart-healthy omega-3 fatty acids than their conventionally produced counterparts.

Of course, since organic produce tends to be more expensive than conventional, you may not be able to go organic all the time. If you are committed to buying organic but are on a budget, I recommend prioritizing based on which foods are most likely to contain pesticide residues. The Environmental Working Group, an advocacy organization that reviews data from the FDA, highlights the fruits and vegetables that are most and least likely to harbor high pesticide loads. First, try to buy organic versions of the foods listed on the Dirty Dozen™ list—these are the produce most impacted by pesticides. Then you can purchase conventionally grown produce that appears on the Clean Fifteen™ list. See the Clean Fifteen™ and the Dirty Dozen Plus™ (page 12) for details.

Organic Labeling

Organic or conventional, there are so many food labels out there, it can be overwhelming and confusing to decipher them all. Here are some of the labels you might see on produce and what you should know about them:

USDA Organic/100% Organic: A product with this label is made entirely of organic ingredients.

SOLID SUCCESS

Once you are ready to start solids, there are a few things you can do to help ensure "solid success." Here are my top 10 strategies for successful feedings.

1. **Start slow**. Begin with just a couple of tablespoons of purée a day. As your baby shows more interest in food, you can gradually increase the number of meals each day, and then the quantity at each meal.

2. **Introduce one food at a time**. Continue each food for two days before trying a new food or adding a spice to the existing food. This way, you'll be able to distinguish preferences, and more importantly, make sure your baby doesn't have an allergic reaction, since it can take a day or two for a rash or other allergy symptoms to appear.

3. **Let baby make a mess**. You want eating to be fun for her. If that means more of the purée ends up on her face than in her tummy, that's fine. That's what bibs and burp cloths (and cameras) are for.

4. **Try, try again**. Don't be discouraged if your baby makes a face or seems to dislike a new food. Children may need to taste a food dozens of times before their taste buds adjust to it, so offer it again a few days later, or mix it with something you know they like.

5. **Develop a routine**. Let your baby try out his new high chair a day or two before you start solids to give him a chance to get comfortable in it. Keep his high chair in the same spot (ideally around your dinner table) so he gets used to the idea that this is where food is served.

6. **Feed solids in between nursings or bottles**. Ideally, you want your baby to be hungry enough to want to eat, but not to the point of melting down. Watch for what works—if your baby is ravenous in the morning, perhaps nurse or bottle-feed first and then try solids one to two hours later.

7. **Don't force it**. If your baby takes a few bites and then turns away from the food or pushes it out of his mouth, that's a good sign that he is either full or done with that particular purée. It's best to end the feeding and try again later.

8. **Start with a plastic bib**. Your baby is bound to make a mess when she first starts solids, so for fast and easy cleanup, use a plastic bib that you can wash in the sink and reuse immediately.

9. **Let your baby lean in for bites**. This cue indicates that your baby is hungry and ready to eat. Resist the urge to push the spoon into your baby's mouth when he's not opening it.

10. **Experiment with the spoon**. She won't be able to feed herself independently at this stage, but once your baby's able to hold it, it's good practice for later, and she'll have fun with it.

Organic: This means that 95 percent of the product's ingredients are organic, while the rest can be non-organic.

Made with Organic Ingredients: This means that at least 70 percent of the ingredients in the product are organic; the rest can be conventional.

Non-GMO Project Verified: GMOs (genetically modified organisms) are plants or animals that have been altered genetically. For example, a plant can be altered to withstand strong pesticides. GMOs are prohibited from certified organic products, which means that organic farmers are not allowed to grow produce from GMO seeds, their animals can't eat GMO feed, and organic food producers can't use GMO ingredients. The Non-GMO Project is a nonprofit organization that independently offers GMO test verification and labeling for non-GMO products. Food products with this label have been tested to ensure that they comply with the guidelines for GMO avoidance.

All Natural: Unfortunately, this label basically means nothing. It's not regulated by the FDA, so any company can label anything *All Natural*. I don't recommend using this as an indicator of the quality of food you're purchasing.

Beyond Produce

I've spent a lot of time talking about organic produce, but the term "organic" can apply to meat, dairy, and oils as well. When it comes to choosing meat and dairy, I usually recommend going organic if you can afford it, but oils are less of a priority if you must make a choice.

Meat: When it comes to meat, look for the labels Organic and Grass Fed. These two labels mean that the animal was raised without any hormones or antibiotics and the food it ate was organic. If the beef you're buying says Grass Fed, the cows were raised on grass instead of feed, which is usually made of corn and other items. Cows' digestive systems are naturally made to digest grass, so it's much harder on their bodies when they have to eat feed. As a result, grass-fed animals have a higher level of healthy fats than animals given a feed-based diet. The nutritional value and flavor of organic, grass-fed meat are much greater than those of conventional meat. For poultry, look for a Free Range label, which is poultry's equivalent of grass fed. Free-range chickens are allowed outside, instead of being kept in cages all day. So the best options are poultry and eggs that have Organic and Free Range labels.

THE CLEAN FIFTEEN™ AND THE DIRTY DOZEN PLUS™

The Environmental Working Group has created two lists of the fruits and vegetables most and least likely to harbor high pesticide loads. If you're committed to buying organic but can't afford to do it all the time, these lists are helpful cheat sheets that will enable you to prioritize your grocery dollars.

THE DIRTY DOZEN™

The Dirty Dozen™ includes the following produce. These are considered among 2018's most important produce to buy organically:

1. Strawberries
2. Apples
3. Nectarines
4. Peaches
5. Celery
6. Grapes
7. Cherries
8. Spinach
9. Tomatoes
10. Bell peppers
11. Cherry tomatoes
12. Cucumbers
    + Kale and collard greens*
    + Hot peppers*

THE CLEAN FIFTEEN™

The least critical to buy organically are the Clean Fifteen™ list. The following are on the list:

1. Avocados
2. Corn
3. Pineapples
4. Cabbage
5. Sweet peas
6. Onions
7. Asparagus
8. Mangos
9. Papayas
10. Kiwi
11. Eggplant
12. Honeydew
13. Grapefruit
14. Cantaloupe
15. Cauliflower

*The Dirty Dozen™ list contains two additional items—kale and collard greens and hot peppers—because they tend to contain trace levels of highly hazardous pesticides.

Dairy : If buying organic is a priority for you, then it's especially important to purchase organic dairy products. When you buy organic milk, you're not only avoiding all the pesticides and synthetic ingredients, but you're also avoiding the hormone given to cows to stimulate milk production (called rBST) and the antibiotics that are fed to cows to keep them from getting sick. Organic dairy cows are not allowed to eat GMO or pesticide-laden feed, so the milk they produce is chemical-free. Ideally, keep an eye out for yogurt and cheese from organic and grass-fed cows.

Oils: Organic oils can be hard to find, but they are out there. Just look for the USDA Organic seal on oils at the store. If you can't find organic oil, it's okay to use conventional since you will likely be using only a very small amount in the food you prepare for your little one.

PLAY WITH YOUR FOOD

● ● ●

Yes, you want baby to get the most nutritious homemade meals possible. But it's equally important that you and your little one are having fun exploring this new world of solid foods. In the first year of life, food is more about allowing children to experiment and taste than straight nutrition—even if that means more food ends up smeared on their faces than in their bellies. This is just an ongoing wonderful photo op that you will laugh about for years to come. Encourage them to explore different flavors and tastes—this will help them develop a healthy and positive relationship with food as they grow older. So, go ahead and feed your children full-flavored foods, particularly when they're toddlers, as this can influence and expand their food preferences later on.

If your child goes through a picky phase, remember that it's just that—a phase—and she will likely get over it. It may take some patience, but you can try mixing the food your child was rejecting with other foods she still likes, or have her take alternate bites between a food she likes and one she's less enthusiastic about. Just don't give up. Keep exposing your child to those flavors; this will encourage her taste buds to adapt. She'll very likely come around sooner or later.

Chapter Two

BABY FOOD MADE EASY

This chapter serves as a guide to making homemade baby food preparation as simple as possible. We'll explore how to keep your pantry stocked (especially for last-minute needs), get the right equipment, and prepare a make-ahead plan so you'll have baby food whenever you need it. You might already have most of the items you need at home, but I'll let you know which tools are most helpful and help you take all the guesswork out of preparing baby's first meals.

PURÉE-READY PANTRY

I'm a planner, so I always liked to make sure my pantry was stocked when I was making baby food for my daughter. With just a little bit of advance thinking, baby food purées are a snap. Here are the items to keep on hand for easy, last-minute meals.

Frozen produce: This is my number one tip when it comes to stocking your pantry. Frozen produce is cheaper than fresh and just as nutritious and delicious. As an added bonus, frozen produce is already chopped and cleaned, so all you have to do is dump it into a pot, steam it, and then purée. The options are nearly infinite, from blueberries, peaches, and strawberries to broccoli, spinach, cauliflower, carrots, green beans, peas, butternut squash, and more. A single trip to the frozen-foods aisle of your grocery store can keep your baby fed for weeks.

Fresh produce: Buy produce that will last a few weeks without spoiling. Bananas, apples, squash, and sweet potatoes are all good options, though you can also freeze most of these if they start getting tired—just peel the banana first.

Canned goods: Chickpeas, beans, and other legumes are essential, since they can be added to any purée to bulk up the protein content.

Herbs and spices: The sky's the limit here, but some of my favorites are cinnamon, allspice, nutmeg, cardamom, ginger, cumin, coriander, turmeric, garlic, garam masala, mint, rosemary, thyme, and oregano.

Nuts and seeds: Since these last just about forever, it's easy to have them on hand. Ground flaxseed and ground chia seeds are particularly useful since they can be easily added to any purée.

PURÉE-MAKING TOOLS AND EQUIPMENT

Cooking baby food is really simple, especially if you have most of the items you need at home. It's as simple as steam, purée, freeze. And while there are lots of dedicated baby food blenders out there, all you need is a really good food processor or blender. Here is a guide to help you get organized for this immensely rewarding activity:

Prep

One good **chopping knife** is enough for all your prep work. If you want to get fancy, you could add one good paring knife for some of those smaller fruits and veggies. I also recommend a couple of sturdy, dishwasher-safe **cutting boards** to make cleanup a snap. **Vegetable peelers** come in handy for fruits and veggies that have hard or inedible peels (think butternut squash, melon, and sweet potatoes). I actually don't recommend peeling fruits or veggies if you are puréeing your baby's food. Many nutrients are contained in the peel, and when you cook it, the peel will simply melt into the purée.

Cook

I recommend having a couple of different-size pots—**one large stockpot, one medium pot**—ideally with **steamer inserts** that fit inside. You can also boil your fruits and veggies without the insert, but if you do that, don't throw out any water the produce is cooked in; instead, use that enriched water in the purée.

Blend

You need a very good **blender** or **food processor**; one that will pulverize foods to a smooth, even consistency. It's worth investing in a good blender because you will be using it all the time and it will cut your prep time significantly. My Vitamix was a lifesaver and worked well with every type of purée, from beans to vegetables to grains and even meats.

Freeze

Though you can find special baby-food **freezer trays**, silicone storage trays or ice cube trays will work just fine. The key is to find a tray with a fitted cover to keep your purées from getting freezer burn. I recommend buying four to six trays, so you always have enough on hand to rotate and freeze your purées.

Store

Airtight **zip-top bags** are ideal for storing your frozen purées. They are affordable, they don't take up a lot of space, and you can easily label them so you know what purées you have in your freezer. Transfer your purées to these bags after they have been frozen for 24 to 48 hours.

Feed

It's worth investing in a few **mesh food feeders**. These are a great place to start before you even delve into purées. You just put a small piece of food inside and your baby can suck on it, getting the taste of the food without any risk of choking. It's also a good idea to purchase a bunch of soft BPA-, phthalate-, and PVC-free **spoons**, since they are much gentler on tender gums than metal spoons. We used OXO brand spoons for our daughter, and opted for plastic BPA-, phthalate-, and PVC-free bowls as well. That way, if she did knock the bowl off her high chair, we didn't have to worry about it breaking.

THE MAKE-AHEAD PURÉE PROCESS

Making baby food at home doesn't have to be time-consuming or difficult. Since your baby will start slowly, with one-ingredient purées, your first few shopping lists will be short ones. Follow this step-by-step make-ahead program, and you can always have at least a six-flavor supply of wholesome baby food at the ready. I would often fit this prep into one weekend each month, and then reap the benefits for weeks afterward.

WITH A LITTLE HELP FROM FRIENDS

● ● ●

Making baby food can be even more fun if you have a little help. If any friends or family ask if you need a hand with anything, suggest that they come over for a baby-food batch-making party. And you might be surprised—enthusiastic friends and family may have suggestions for food combinations that you hadn't thought of before. You can ask them to buy groceries, help with some of the cutting and chopping prep, or even work a little assembly line where one person is cutting and steaming, and another is puréeing and freezing. In just an hour or two, you will end up with enough baby food to last you over a month. If you have other like-minded friends with babies, you may even want to consider a baby-food swap. Each parent makes some large batches of one or two purées, labels them with the ingredients and date of preparation, and then swaps with others to build a varied supply of delicious and healthy baby food for each family.

Step 1: Create a Menu

Start by selecting six purées that you'd like your baby to try. If you need some inspiration, you'll find 30 single-ingredient purées in chapter 3 that you can pick and choose from. With Layla, I always kept avocados, apples, pears, sweet potatoes, green beans, carrots, broccoli, cauliflower, spinach, and lentils on hand since those became her favorites. You can prepare batches of these purées in under two hours and freeze them for a month-long supply.

When you choose your purées, aim for the widest possible variety of colors and flavors. As you consider your options, try to pick flavors that will work well together if you choose to combine purées later (e.g., apple and sweet potato work well together, as do pear and spinach). The Purée Mix-and-Match Chart (page 102) offers some pointers on successful flavor combos.

Here are four sample menus you can start with:

MENU 1:

APPLE PURÉE, page 32
APRICOT PURÉE, page 35
BUTTERNUT SQUASH PURÉE, page 47
PEAR PURÉE, page 37
SPINACH PURÉE, page 52
ZUCCHINI PURÉE, page 44

MENU 2:

AVOCADO PURÉE, page 40
CARROT PURÉE, page 41
CAULIFLOWER PURÉE, page 50
GREEN BEAN PURÉE, page 45
LENTIL PURÉE, page 57
PEACH PURÉE, page 36

MENU 3:

BANANA PURÉE, page 31
BLUEBERRY PURÉE, page 34
BUTTERNUT SQUASH PURÉE, page 47
OATMEAL PURÉE, page 55
SWEET POTATO PURÉE, page 48
ZUCCHINI PURÉE, page 44

MENU 4:

APPLE PURÉE, page 32
BEEF PURÉE, page 63
BROCCOLI PURÉE, page 54
CARROT PURÉE, page 41
GREEN BEAN PURÉE, page 45
PEAR PURÉE, page 37

Step 2: Make a Shopping List

What's in season? When considering what fresh produce to buy, look to seasonal options; those purées will taste better and be less expensive, too. This strategy doesn't apply to frozen items since those crops are picked and flash frozen when they are in peak season.

I like to organize my shopping list by areas of the store: fresh produce, frozen foods, dry foods, dairy, meat, and other. I then highlight the items I want to buy organic, as well as the items I plan to buy in the frozen section (most fruits and vegetables work great frozen if you are using them in purées).

If you plan to use the menus in Step 1, you can simply use the following shopping lists. An asterisk (*) indicates a produce item most worth buying organic based on the Clean Fifteen™ and the Dirty Dozen Plus™ list (page 12).

MENU 1:

FRESH PRODUCE: Apples* (4), apricots (1½ lbs.), pears (4), zucchini (1½ lbs.)
FROZEN FOODS: Butternut squash (16 oz.), spinach* (16 oz.)

MENU 2:

FRESH PRODUCE: Avocados (3), peaches* (1½ lbs.)
FROZEN FOODS: Carrots (16 oz.), cauliflower (16 oz.), green beans (16 oz.)
DRY FOODS: Lentils (1 cup)

MENU 3:

FRESH PRODUCE: Bananas (3), sweet potatoes (3), zucchini (1½ lbs.)
FROZEN FOODS: Blueberries (16 oz.), butternut squash (16 oz.)
DRY FOODS: Rolled oats (½ cup)

MENU 4:

FRESH PRODUCE: Apples* (4), pears* (4)
FROZEN FOODS: Broccoli (16 oz.), carrots (16 oz.), green beans (16 oz.)
MEAT: Lean beef (8 oz.)

Step 3: Purchase Foods

Now that you have your list ready to go, head to your local market to pick up all of your ingredients. But wait—before you go, make sure you have enough space in your refrigerator and freezer for all of your groceries. It may seem like you're buying a lot of food, but remember, this plan is designed to last you several weeks. And feel free to improvise if you see an abundance of fruits and vegetables at their peak. If it's peak blueberry season, take full advantage!

Step 4: Prep the Kitchen

You are ready to start cooking, so let's discuss how to create the perfect work-space in your kitchen for your baby-food batch sessions. First, make sure your ice cube trays are clean and ready to go, and make room in your freezer to place these trays. Then clear and clean your counter space where you will prep the ingredients, and take out all of your prepping and cooking equipment. Finally, line up all of the colorful and nutritious ingredients you'll be using, so you know they're there, ready for you to make them into the best baby food ever, with love.

TOOLS YOU'LL NEED:

- Blender or food processor
- Chef's knife
- Colander
- Cutting board
- Freezer storage bags, 1-quart
- 6 freezer trays, silicone, 15 (1-ounce) cubes
- Paring knife or vegetable peeler
- Prep bowls
- Small pot with lid
- Steamer
- Parchment paper

Step 5: No-Cook Purées

No-cook purées are the quickest and easiest of the recipes I'll be showing you. Simply wash and chop your fruit or veggie of choice, dump it into your high-quality blender, and blend until smooth throughout. Then pour the purée into your ice cube trays and transfer to the freezer. Done. I always start with avocados since those seem to spoil first, followed by mangos and melons, then tofu, and finally bananas, since those last the longest on my counter.

Step 6: Cooked Purées

For cooked purées, I recommend starting with the ones that have to cook the longest. These include grains, legumes, or any squashes or foods you plan on roasting. To save time, cut larger fruits or veggies into smaller chunks so they cook more quickly. Once those are underway, you can turn your attention to heating up frozen produce that is precut and steams quickly. If you are steaming your veggies or fruit, you probably won't have to clean your pot in between steaming sessions since the food won't be touching the bottom.

Once you have made your purées, pour them into ice cube trays and freeze for at least 24 hours. Once they're solid, you can transfer them into zip-top storage bags. Label the bags with the purée name, date cooked/packed, and shelf life (almost all purées will last for six months in the freezer). Whatever you do, make sure it's easy to see the date, so you can use the oldest purées first. If you're super organized, you may want to divide your fruits and veggies into separate bins.

RECIPE ....

DATE COOKED/PACKED ....

SHELF LIFE ....

THAWING AND SERVING PURÉES

You have all of your baby food labeled neatly in the freezer—so how do you get those frozen purée cubes ready for baby? If you're planning ahead for the next day, just place the frozen purée cubes in a covered container in the refrigerator overnight to thaw. In the morning, you can heat them on the stovetop or in the microwave. However, if your baby is starving and shouting the equivalent of "Feed me now!" you can always go straight from freezer to microwave in a pinch. To quick-thaw frozen purée cubes in the microwave, place them in a glass container and use your microwave's defrost setting to thaw the cubes evenly. You can also thaw the cubes on your stovetop—just be sure to do so over low heat. Aim for a little above room temperature. Test it out on your tongue before feeding it to your baby—it should feel slightly warm but not hot (about the same temperature you'd heat a bottle to). In all cases, definitely be sure to give your purées a good stir to make sure they have heated up evenly. Then transfer the food to a plastic bowl (ideally, BPA-free and microwave-safe) and serve.

FOOD SAFETY PRACTICES

Food safety is important when preparing all foods at home and could never be more so than when making food for your little one. Here are a few food safety tips to keep your baby safe and healthy:

- Thoroughly wash your hands and all equipment before cooking your baby's food.

- Use one cutting board for meat, poultry, and fish, and a separate one for non-meat foods to avoid cross-contamination.

- Wash fresh fruits and vegetables thoroughly. Even if you plan to peel a fruit or vegetable, wash it first—bacteria collects on skins and rinds, and the knife can transfer this bacteria onto the produce.

- Cook meat, poultry, and fish thoroughly to kill any bacteria that might be present. Use a meat thermometer and cook red meat to an internal temperature of at least 160°F, fish to at least 145°F, and white-meat poultry to at least 165°F. Frozen, previously cooked meats should be reheated to those temperatures after thawing.

- Never allow cooked food to stand at room temperature for more than 2 hours (or more than 1 hour when the room temperature is above 90°F).

- Freeze all baby food immediately after preparing it.

- Never thaw frozen baby foods by leaving them at room temperature or in standing water.

MEAL PLANNING

As you start creating meal plans for your baby, it's important to start off slowly. For all the good reasons we've discussed, babies should begin by eating just one solid food per day, one time per day, and eventually work their way up to three solid-food meals a day. For instance, during those first weeks, your meal plan might consist of avocado and sweet potato all week long. (Baby's First Spoonful, page 4, is a great place to start if you're looking for guidance for your little one's first meals.) As your baby gets used to purées, it's time to begin varying your meal plans to expose her to an increasing assortment of flavors. That might mean a combination of blueberry and oatmeal purées for breakfast, green bean and sweet potato purées for lunch, and lentil and spinach purées for dinner.

Here is a four-week plan using sample menus 1 and 2 (page 19) for your baby's first month of solid food. To create variety, simply mix the different single-ingredient purées together in the following combinations suggested in equal proportions (for example, for the Apple and Carrot Purée, mix 1 ounce Apple Purée, page 32, with 1 ounce Carrot Purée, page 41). Or change up these menus to your and your little one's liking. Just remember to wait two days before introducing new foods to ensure your baby's system can tolerate them.

	DAY 1	DAY 2	DAY 3	DAY 4
WEEK 1	Avocado Purée (PAGE 40)	Avocado Purée (PAGE 40)	Avocado Purée (PAGE 40)	Sweet Potato Purée (PAGE 48)
	DAY 5	**DAY 6**		**DAY 7**
	Sweet Potato Purée (PAGE 48)	Sweet Potato Purée (PAGE 48)		Peach Purée (PAGE 36)

	DAY 1	DAY 2	DAY 3	DAY 4
WEEK 2	Peach Purée (PAGE 36)	Peach Purée (PAGE 36)	Carrot Purée (PAGE 41)	Carrot Purée (PAGE 41)
	DAY 5	**DAY 6**		**DAY 7**
	Carrot Purée (PAGE 41)	Green Bean Purée (PAGE 45)		Green Bean Purée (PAGE 45)

	DAY 1	DAY 2	DAY 3	DAY 4
WEEK 3	Green Bean Purée (PAGE 45)	Apple Purée (PAGE 32)	Apple Purée (PAGE 32)	Apple Purée (PAGE 32)

	DAY 5	DAY 6	DAY 7
WEEK 3	Apricot Purée (PAGE 35)	Apricot Purée (PAGE 35)	Apricot Purée (PAGE 35)

	DAY 1	DAY 2	DAY 3	DAY 4
WEEK 4	**MEAL 1:** Peach and Banana Purée (PAGES 36 AND 31) **MEAL 2:** Apple and Carrot Purée with Cinammon (PAGES 32 AND 41)	**MEAL 1:** Carrot Purée (PAGE 41) **MEAL 2:** Apple and Carrot Purée (PAGES 32 AND 41)	**MEAL 1:** Avocado Purée (PAGE 40) **MEAL 2:** Avocado and Spinach Purée (PAGES 40 AND 52)	**MEAL 1:** Avocado Purée (PAGE 40) **MEAL 2:** Avocado and Spinach Purée (PAGES 40 AND 52)

	DAY 5	DAY 6	DAY 7
WEEK 4	**MEAL 1:** Pear and Spinach Purée (PAGES 37 AND 52) **MEAL 2:** Avocado and Spinach Purée (PAGES 40 AND 52)	**MEAL 1:** Apple, Spinach, and Avocado Purée (PAGES 32, 52, AND 40) **MEAL 2:** Lentil Purée (PAGE 57)	**MEAL 1:** Pear and Spinach Purée (PAGES 37 AND 52) **MEAL 2:** Apple and Carrot Purée (PAGES 32 AND 41)

PART TWO

RECIPES FOR BABY

Blueberry Purée, page 34

Chapter Three

SINGLE-INGREDIENT PURÉES

6 MONTHS

Whether your baby is four months old (the earliest a baby can start solids) or six months old (the age most pediatricians recommend), this is an exciting new experience. Initially, you can offer solids once a day: about 1 tablespoon of puréed food thinned with water, breast milk, or formula. You want the purée to be thin enough so that your baby doesn't gag, since this is new to him. In fact, all he is used to is milk so far! As long as your baby continues to open his mouth or lean forward for bites, keep feeding him. Once your baby pushes the spoon away with his mouth, tongue, or hand, or turns his head away from the food, you can take that as a cue that he is done for now. Quantity matters less than frequency at this stage, because your baby is still getting most of his nutrition from breast milk or formula. For now, just keep offering a variety of foods, and eventually your baby will adjust.

WHAT'S ON THE TABLE
6 MONTHS

HOW OFTEN: Once per day initially

WHAT TO EAT: One single-ingredient purée

HOW MUCH: 1 to 2 tablespoons

FINGER FOODS: None

WHAT TO DRINK: Water; 24 to 40 ounces of breast milk or formula in between meals

BANANA PURÉE

• • •

YIELD: 15 (1-OUNCE) FREEZER CUBES   **PREP TIME:** 5 MINUTES

I don't think I've met a baby who doesn't like banana. It's a perennial crowd-pleaser, thanks to its sweetness and soft texture. It's also one of the few no-cook purées out there, making it a snap to prepare at home. Bananas are high in potassium and vitamin C.

❄️
FREEZER-FRIENDLY

🥛
DAIRY-FREE

🌾
GLUTEN-FREE

🥜
NUT-FREE

Ⓥ
VEGAN

🆅🅶
VEGETARIAN

3 bananas, peeled

1 tablespoon water, plus more if needed

1. In a high-speed blender, blend the bananas and water with a pinch of herb or spice (if using), until combined. Add more water to achieve your desired texture.

2. Transfer to ice cube trays and freeze.

STORAGE: Freeze overnight, then transfer the frozen cubes to a gallon-size, airtight zip-top bag. Purées will last in the freezer for up to 6 months; they can be thawed in the refrigerator overnight or in the microwave on the defrost setting.

HERBS AND SPICES: Bananas are delicious with warm spices like cinnamon, nutmeg, allspice, cardamom, and ginger.

APPLE PURÉE

• • •

YIELD: 15 (1-OUNCE) FREEZER CUBES   **PREP TIME:** 5 MINUTES   **COOK TIME:** 10 TO 15 MINUTES

Apples are easy for babies to digest and not too sweet. I recommend leaving the skin on for this purée, because the skin becomes incredibly soft and blends easily once it's been cooked down, allowing you to retain all of its nutrients.

FREEZER-FRIENDLY

DAIRY-FREE

GLUTEN-FREE

NUT-FREE

VEGAN

VEGETARIAN

4 Fuji apples (or any apple you like), cored and cut into 1-inch cubes

¼ cup water, plus more if needed

1. Pour about ½ inch of water into a medium pot and set a steamer basket inside it. Arrange the apples evenly inside the basket. Bring to a simmer over medium heat and steam for 10 to 15 minutes, until the apples are soft (cover the pot to speed up the cooking time).

2. Transfer the cooked apples and steaming water to a blender. (Add more water as needed; start by adding a little bit at a time, since you can always add more.)

3. Add a pinch of herb or spice (if using).

4. Blend until combined and very smooth.

5. Transfer the purée to ice cube trays and freeze.

STORAGE: Freeze overnight, then transfer the frozen cubes to a gallon-size, airtight zip-top bag. Purées will last in the freezer for up to 6 months; they can be thawed in the refrigerator overnight or in the microwave on the defrost setting.

HERBS AND SPICES: Apples work well with familiar sweet spices like cinnamon, nutmeg, cloves, ginger, and cardamom.

BLUEBERRY PURÉE

• • •

YIELD: 15 (1-OUNCE) FREEZER CUBES   **PREP TIME:** 5 MINUTES   **COOK TIME:** 10 TO 20 MINUTES

Blueberries (and all berries, really) are high in antioxidants, fiber, and loads of other nutrients, so you can use any berries you like, in the same proportions—for example, swap out the blueberries for 1½ pounds of strawberries, hulled and halved. Some berries are more allergenic than others, though, so it's always a good idea to introduce each type of berry separately and then watch for a reaction within two days, to ensure your baby doesn't have any issues with them.

FREEZER-FRIENDLY

DAIRY-FREE

GLUTEN-FREE

NUT-FREE

V

VEGAN

VG

VEGETARIAN

1½ pounds fresh blueberries (or 1 [16-ounce] package frozen blueberries)

¼ cup water, plus more if needed

1. Pour about ½ inch of water into a medium pot and set a steamer basket inside it. Arrange the blueberries evenly inside the basket. Bring to a simmer over medium heat and steam for 10 to 20 minutes, until the berries are soft (cover the pot to speed up the cooking time).

2. Transfer the cooked blueberries and steaming water to a blender.

3. Add a pinch of herb or spice, if using.

4. Blend until combined and very smooth. (Add more water as needed; start by adding a little bit at a time, since you can always add more.)

5. Transfer the purée to ice cube trays and freeze.

STORAGE: Freeze overnight, then transfer the frozen cubes to a gallon-size, airtight zip-top bag. Purées will last in the freezer for up to 6 months; they can be thawed in the refrigerator overnight or in the microwave on the defrost setting.

HERBS AND SPICES: Cinnamon, cardamom, nutmeg, allspice, and ginger are delicious with blueberries—but you can also try savory herb combinations like mint, basil, and rosemary.

APRICOT PURÉE

· · ·

YIELD: 15 (1-OUNCE) FREEZER CUBES   **PREP TIME:** 10 MINUTES   **COOK TIME:** 10 TO 15 MINUTES

Apricots are delicious, sweet fruits readily available in the summer. They are an excellent source of vitamins A and C, copper, dietary fiber, and potassium. Be sure you take the pit out of the apricot before puréeing, but feel free to leave the skins on, since they will soften when you steam the fruit.

FREEZER-FRIENDLY

DAIRY-FREE

GLUTEN-FREE

NUT-FREE

(V)

VEGAN

VEGETARIAN

1½ pounds apricots, halved and pitted

¼ cup water, plus more if needed

1. Pour about ½ inch of water into a medium pot and set a steamer basket inside it. Arrange the apricots evenly inside the basket. Bring to a simmer over medium heat and steam for 10 to 15 minutes, until the apricots are soft (cover the pot to speed up the cooking time).

2. Transfer the cooked apricots and steaming water to a blender.

3. Add a pinch of herb or spice (if using).

4. Blend until combined and very smooth. (Add more water as needed; start by adding a little bit at a time, since you can always add more.)

5. Transfer the purée to ice cube trays and freeze.

STORAGE: Freeze overnight, then transfer the frozen cubes to a gallon-size, airtight zip-top bag. Purées will last in the freezer for up to 6 months; they can be thawed in the refrigerator overnight or in the microwave on the defrost setting.

HERBS AND SPICES: Apricots and warm spices are a classic combination, so try using nutmeg, cinnamon, allspice, or cardamom. Having said that, they go really well with fresh herbs like basil and mint, too.

PEACH PURÉE

• • •

YIELD: 15 (1-OUNCE) FREEZER CUBES   **PREP TIME:** 5 MINUTES   **COOK TIME:** 10 TO 15 MINUTES

I absolutely love fresh peaches in the summer when stone fruits are in season, but you can also find frozen peaches any time of year. I recommend keeping the skins on, because the skins will become soft enough to melt into your purée once you cook them down—and that way you'll retain all of the nutrients contained in the skin.

FREEZER-FRIENDLY

DAIRY-FREE

GLUTEN-FREE

NUT-FREE

VEGAN

VEGETARIAN

1½ pounds fresh peaches, pitted and cut into 1-inch cubes (or 1 [16-ounce] package frozen peaches, thawed)

¼ cup water, plus more if needed

1. Pour about ½ inch of water into a medium pot and set a steamer basket inside it. Arrange the peaches evenly inside the basket. Bring to a simmer over medium heat and steam for 10 to 15 minutes, until the peaches are soft (cover the pot to speed up the cooking time).

2. Transfer the cooked peaches and steaming water to a blender.

3. Add a pinch of herb or spice (if using).

4. Blend until combined and very smooth. (Add more water as needed; start by adding a little bit at a time, since you can always add more.)

5. Transfer the purée to ice cube trays and freeze.

STORAGE: Freeze overnight, then transfer the frozen cubes to a gallon-size, airtight zip-top bag. Purées will last in the freezer for up to 6 months; they can be thawed in the refrigerator overnight or in the microwave on the defrost setting.

HERBS AND SPICES: Peaches pair well with just about any spice. Warm spices—like cinnamon, cloves, and nutmeg—work great, but so do savory flavors such as basil, mint, thyme, and rosemary.

PEAR PURÉE

● ● ●

YIELD: 15 (1-OUNCE) FREEZER CUBES   **PREP TIME:** 5 MINUTES   **COOK TIME:** 10 TO 15 MINUTES

Layla absolutely loved pear purée, probably because of its mild, sweet flavor. I recommend leaving the skin on to retain all of the nutrients. When cooked down, the skin becomes soft enough to blend evenly into the purée.

FREEZER-FRIENDLY

DAIRY-FREE

GLUTEN-FREE

NUT-FREE

VEGAN

VEGETARIAN

4 Bartlett pears (or any pear you like), cored and cut into 1-inch cubes

¼ cup water, plus more if needed

1. Pour about ½ inch of water into a medium pot and set a steamer basket inside it. Arrange the pears evenly inside the basket. Bring to a simmer over medium heat and steam for 10 to 15 minutes, until the pears are soft (cover the pot to speed up the cooking time).

2. Transfer the cooked pears and steaming water to a blender.

3. Add a pinch of herb or spice (if using).

4. Blend until combined and very smooth. (Add more water as needed; start by adding a little bit at a time, since you can always add more.)

5. Transfer the purée to ice cube trays and freeze.

STORAGE: Freeze overnight, then transfer the frozen cubes to a gallon-size, airtight zip-top bag. Purées will last in the freezer for up to 6 months; they can be thawed in the refrigerator overnight or in the microwave on the defrost setting.

HERBS AND SPICES: Pears taste great with cinnamon, nutmeg, star anise, ginger, cardamom, and cloves.

MANGO PURÉE

• • •

YIELD: 15 (1-OUNCE) FREEZER CUBES **PREP TIME:** 5 MINUTES

When mangos are ripe they can be very sweet, which makes them a nice "treat" for your baby. They are also an excellent source of fiber, folate, and vitamins A and C. Getting all the fruit off the flat, odd-shaped pit can take some practice, but the payoff is proven by this fruit's worldwide popularity.

FREEZER-FRIENDLY

DAIRY-FREE

GLUTEN-FREE

NUT-FREE

(V)

VEGAN

(VG)

VEGETARIAN

1½ pounds fresh mango, peeled, pitted, and cut into 1-inch cubes (or 1 [16-ounce] package frozen mango, thawed)

½ cup water, plus more if needed

1. In a high-speed blender, blend the mango and water, with a pinch of herb or spice (if using), until combined. Add more water to achieve your desired texture.

2. Transfer to ice cube trays and freeze.

STORAGE: Freeze overnight, then transfer the frozen cubes to a gallon-size, airtight zip-top bag. Purées will last in the freezer for up to 6 months; they can be thawed in the refrigerator overnight or in the microwave on the defrost setting.

HERBS AND SPICES: Mango pairs well with cumin, coriander, cinnamon, ginger, allspice, and nutmeg.

PRUNE PURÉE

• • •

YIELD: 15 (1-OUNCE) FREEZER CUBES **PREP TIME:** 35 MINUTES

This is one of my favorite purées to keep things "moving" for baby. If your baby is having trouble with constipation, which can happen with the transition to solids, offer your child 1 tablespoon Prune Purée and 1 tablespoon Apple Purée (page 32) mixed with 1 tablespoon Oatmeal Purée (page 55) or yogurt. Feel free to increase the amount of prune purée depending on how constipated your baby is.

FREEZER-FRIENDLY

DAIRY-FREE

GLUTEN-FREE

NUT-FREE

V

VEGAN

VG

VEGETARIAN

2 cups dried, pitted prunes (with no sugar or oils added)

1 cup boiling water (or enough to cover the prunes)

1. Put the prunes in a large glass or metal bowl and add boiling water (just enough to cover the prunes). Cover the bowl and let sit for 30 minutes.

2. In a high-speed blender, blend the prunes and water, with a pinch of herb or spice (if using), until combined. Add more water to achieve your desired texture.

3. Transfer to ice cube trays and freeze.

STORAGE: Freeze overnight, then transfer the frozen cubes to a gallon-size, airtight zip-top bag. Purées will last in the freezer for up to 6 months; they can be thawed in the refrigerator overnight or in the microwave on the defrost setting.

HERBS AND SPICES: Prunes taste great with cinnamon, allspice, and cloves, but you can also try a pinch of thyme (fresh leaves are especially good with prunes) for a delicious, savory flavor.

AVOCADO PURÉE

• • •

YIELD: 15 (1-OUNCE) FREEZER CUBES   **PREP TIME:** 5 MINUTES

Avocados are a great first food for your little one, because they are creamy and mild in flavor and require no cooking. They are also full of healthy fats and high in vitamins A and C.

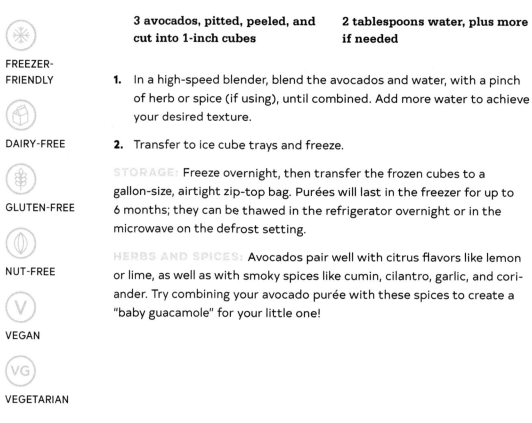

FREEZER-FRIENDLY

DAIRY-FREE

GLUTEN-FREE

NUT-FREE

VEGAN

VEGETARIAN

3 avocados, pitted, peeled, and cut into 1-inch cubes

2 tablespoons water, plus more if needed

1. In a high-speed blender, blend the avocados and water, with a pinch of herb or spice (if using), until combined. Add more water to achieve your desired texture.

2. Transfer to ice cube trays and freeze.

STORAGE: Freeze overnight, then transfer the frozen cubes to a gallon-size, airtight zip-top bag. Purées will last in the freezer for up to 6 months; they can be thawed in the refrigerator overnight or in the microwave on the defrost setting.

HERBS AND SPICES: Avocados pair well with citrus flavors like lemon or lime, as well as with smoky spices like cumin, cilantro, garlic, and coriander. Try combining your avocado purée with these spices to create a "baby guacamole" for your little one!

CARROT PURÉE

• • •

YIELD: 15 (1-OUNCE) FREEZER CUBES   **PREP TIME:** 10 MINUTES   **COOK TIME:** 10 TO 15 MINUTES

Most babies love carrots because of their mild, sweet flavor. They are high in beta-carotene, vitamins A and C, and calcium. Make sure to get full-size carrots (not baby carrots) when making this purée for full nutritional impact and to avoid any added processing that might occur when turning regular-size carrots into their baby variety.

FREEZER-
FRIENDLY

DAIRY-FREE

GLUTEN-FREE

NUT-FREE

VEGAN

VG

VEGETARIAN

1½ pounds carrots, peeled and cut into 1-inch cubes

¼ cup water, plus more if needed

1. Pour about ½ inch of water into a medium pot and set a steamer basket inside it. Arrange the carrots evenly inside the basket. Bring to a simmer over medium heat and steam for 10 to 15 minutes, until the carrots are soft (cover the pot to speed up the cooking time).

2. Transfer the cooked carrots and steaming water to a blender.

3. Add a pinch of herb or spice (if using).

4. Blend until combined and very smooth. (Add more water as needed; start by adding a little bit at a time, since you can always add more.)

5. Transfer the purée to ice cube trays and freeze.

STORAGE: Freeze overnight, then transfer the frozen cubes to a gallon-size, airtight zip-top bag. Purées will last in the freezer for up to 6 months; they can be thawed in the refrigerator overnight or in the microwave on the defrost setting.

HERBS AND SPICES: Sweet spices, like cinnamon, allspice, cloves, and nutmeg, work well with carrots. But carrots are also delicious with savory spices like cumin and coriander, or herbs like thyme or oregano.

RED BELL PEPPER PURÉE

• • •

YIELD: 15 (1-OUNCE) FREEZER CUBES   **PREP TIME:** 10 MINUTES   **COOK TIME:** 10 TO 20 MINUTES

Loaded with folate, vitamin A (from beta-carotene), vitamin B$_6$, and vitamin C, red bell peppers pack a nutritional wallop. Feel free to substitute any color of bell pepper here, but keep in mind that red, yellow, and orange peppers are the sweetest and mildest in flavor.

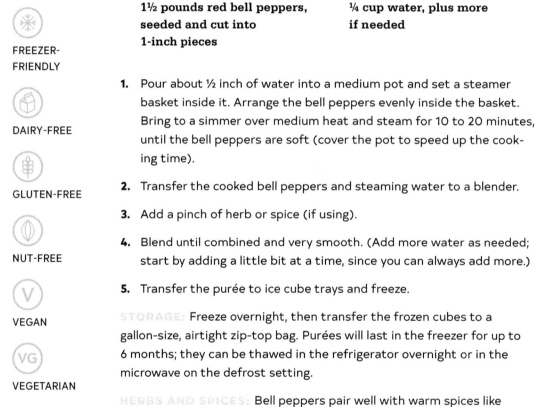

FREEZER-FRIENDLY

DAIRY-FREE

GLUTEN-FREE

NUT-FREE

VEGAN

VG VEGETARIAN

1½ pounds red bell peppers, seeded and cut into 1-inch pieces

¼ cup water, plus more if needed

1. Pour about ½ inch of water into a medium pot and set a steamer basket inside it. Arrange the bell peppers evenly inside the basket. Bring to a simmer over medium heat and steam for 10 to 20 minutes, until the bell peppers are soft (cover the pot to speed up the cooking time).

2. Transfer the cooked bell peppers and steaming water to a blender.

3. Add a pinch of herb or spice (if using).

4. Blend until combined and very smooth. (Add more water as needed; start by adding a little bit at a time, since you can always add more.)

5. Transfer the purée to ice cube trays and freeze.

STORAGE: Freeze overnight, then transfer the frozen cubes to a gallon-size, airtight zip-top bag. Purées will last in the freezer for up to 6 months; they can be thawed in the refrigerator overnight or in the microwave on the defrost setting.

HERBS AND SPICES: Bell peppers pair well with warm spices like cumin, coriander, and garlic, but they also work beautifully with earthy herbs such as oregano and basil.

BEET PURÉE

● ● ●

YIELD: 15 (1-OUNCE) FREEZER CUBES   **PREP TIME:** 10 MINUTES   **COOK TIME:** 10 TO 20 MINUTES

Beets are naturally sweet and high in calcium, potassium, and vitamin A. I love combining vibrant beet purée with both veggie and fruit purées, since their sweetness pairs well with fruits and cuts some of the stronger flavors in veggie purées.

FREEZER-
FRIENDLY

DAIRY-FREE

GLUTEN-FREE

NUT-FREE

VEGAN

VG

VEGETARIAN

1½ pounds beets, peeled and cut into 1-inch cubes

¼ cup water, plus more if needed

1. Pour about ½ inch of water into a medium pot and set a steamer basket inside it. Arrange the beets evenly inside the basket. Bring to a simmer over medium heat and steam for 10 to 20 minutes until the beets are soft (cover the pot to speed up the cooking time).

2. Transfer the cooked beets and steaming water to a blender.

3. Add a pinch of herb or spice (if using).

4. Blend until combined and very smooth. (Add more water as needed; start by adding a little bit at a time, since you can always add more.)

5. Transfer the purée to ice cube trays and freeze.

STORAGE: Freeze overnight, then transfer the frozen cubes to a gallon-size, airtight zip-top bag. Purées will last in the freezer for up to 6 months; they can be thawed in the refrigerator overnight or in the microwave on the defrost setting.

HERBS AND SPICES: Beets are sweet and earthy. They pair well with spicy, fragrant, and warm herbs and spices. Try basil, cloves, coriander, cumin, ginger, fennel, allspice, sage, thyme, and tarragon.

ZUCCHINI PURÉE

• • •

YIELD: 15 (1-OUNCE) FREEZER CUBES   **PREP TIME:** 10 MINUTES   **COOK TIME:** 10 TO 15 MINUTES

Zucchini are most flavorful in the summer months, but you can usually find zucchini year-round. Zucchini skin is very delicate, which means you don't have to worry about peeling this squash before cooking it for your baby. This recipe works equally well with other summer squashes.

FREEZER-FRIENDLY

DAIRY-FREE

GLUTEN-FREE

NUT-FREE

VEGAN

VG

VEGETARIAN

1½ pounds zucchini (or any soft-skinned summer squash, such as yellow squash), cut into 1-inch cubes

¼ cup water, plus more if needed

1. Pour about ½ inch of water into a medium pot and set a steamer basket inside it. Arrange the zucchini evenly inside the basket. Bring to a simmer over medium heat and steam for 10 to 15 minutes until the zucchini is soft (cover the pot to speed up the cooking time).

2. Transfer the cooked zucchini and steaming water to a blender.

3. Add a pinch of herb or spice (if using).

4. Blend until combined and very smooth. (Add more water as needed; start by adding a little bit at a time, since you can always add more.)

5. Transfer the purée to ice cube trays and freeze.

STORAGE: Freeze overnight, then transfer the frozen cubes to a gallon-size, airtight zip-top bag. Purées will last in the freezer for up to 6 months; they can be thawed in the refrigerator overnight or in the microwave on the defrost setting.

HERBS AND SPICES: Zucchini and other summer squashes go great with garlic, oregano, rosemary, and thyme.

GREEN BEAN PURÉE

• • •

YIELD: 15 (1-OUNCE) FREEZER CUBES   **PREP TIME:** 5 MINUTES   **COOK TIME:** 10 TO 15 MINUTES

Green beans are packed with fiber and vitamin C, which makes them a very healthy choice for your baby. Since green beans can have a tougher skin, I recommend cooking them until they are extremely soft to ensure your purée turns out super smooth. Layla loved green beans mixed with plain whole-milk yogurt; the yogurt helped her adjust to the stronger taste of this green veggie.

FREEZER-FRIENDLY

DAIRY-FREE

GLUTEN-FREE

NUT-FREE

(V)

VEGAN

(VG)

VEGETARIAN

1 (16-ounce) package frozen green beans

¼ cup water, plus more if needed

1. Pour about ½ inch of water into a medium pot and set a steamer basket inside it. Arrange the green beans evenly inside the basket. Bring to a simmer over medium heat and steam for 10 to 15 minutes, until the green beans are soft (cover the pot to speed up the cooking time).

2. Transfer the cooked green beans and steaming water to a blender.

3. Add a pinch of herb or spice (if using).

4. Blend until combined and very smooth. (Add more water as needed; start by adding a little bit at a time, since you can always add more.)

5. Transfer the purée to ice cube trays and freeze.

STORAGE: Freeze overnight, then transfer the frozen cubes to a gallon-size, airtight zip-top bag. Purées will last in the freezer for up to 6 months; they can be thawed in the refrigerator overnight or in the microwave on the defrost setting.

HERBS AND SPICES: Green beans go well with garlic or herbs like rosemary, oregano, and thyme.

BUTTERNUT SQUASH PURÉE

● ● ●

YIELD: 15 (1-OUNCE) FREEZER CUBES **PREP TIME:** 15 MINUTES **COOK TIME:** 10 TO 20 MINUTES

This slightly sweet, nutty, smooth squash is usually a hit with babies. It's also high in vitamins A and C. While roasting butternut squash brings out additional sweetness, I recommend steaming it to save time. If you need to save even more time, you can use 1 (16-ounce) package of frozen butternut squash. Cook the raw, frozen cubes just as you would the fresh version.

FREEZER-FRIENDLY

DAIRY-FREE

GLUTEN-FREE

NUT-FREE

VEGAN

VEGETARIAN

1½ pounds butternut squash (or any hard-skinned squash), peeled, seeded, and cut into 1-inch cubes

¼ cup water, plus more if needed

1. Pour about ½ inch of water into a medium pot and set a steamer basket inside it. Arrange the squash evenly inside the basket. Bring the water to a simmer over medium heat and steam for 10 to 20 minutes, until the squash is soft (cover the pot to speed up the cooking time).

2. Transfer the cooked squash and steaming water to a blender.

3. Add a pinch of herb or spice (if using).

4. Blend until combined and very smooth. (Add more water as needed; start by adding a little bit at a time, since you can always add more.)

5. Transfer the purée to ice cube trays and freeze.

STORAGE: Freeze overnight, then transfer the frozen cubes to a gallon-size, airtight zip-top bag. Purées will last in the freezer for up to 6 months; they can be thawed in the refrigerator overnight or in the microwave on the defrost setting.

HERBS AND SPICES: Try sweet spices like nutmeg and cinnamon, savory spices like cumin and coriander, or savory herbs such as rosemary and thyme.

SWEET POTATO PURÉE

• • •

YIELD: 15 (1-OUNCE) FREEZER CUBES   PREP TIME: 10 MINUTES   COOK TIME: 10 TO 20 MINUTES

Sweet potatoes can be a wonderful first food for your baby since they have a rich, sweet flavor, and your reward is knowing this great flavor comes with high fiber, vitamins A and E, beta-carotene, potassium, calcium, and folate.

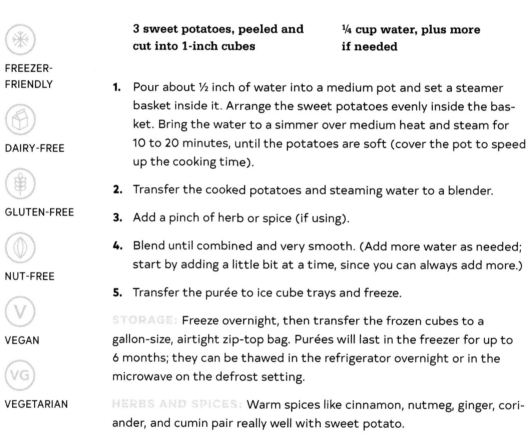

FREEZER-FRIENDLY

DAIRY-FREE

GLUTEN-FREE

NUT-FREE

VEGAN

VEGETARIAN

3 sweet potatoes, peeled and cut into 1-inch cubes

¼ cup water, plus more if needed

1. Pour about ½ inch of water into a medium pot and set a steamer basket inside it. Arrange the sweet potatoes evenly inside the basket. Bring the water to a simmer over medium heat and steam for 10 to 20 minutes, until the potatoes are soft (cover the pot to speed up the cooking time).

2. Transfer the cooked potatoes and steaming water to a blender.

3. Add a pinch of herb or spice (if using).

4. Blend until combined and very smooth. (Add more water as needed; start by adding a little bit at a time, since you can always add more.)

5. Transfer the purée to ice cube trays and freeze.

STORAGE: Freeze overnight, then transfer the frozen cubes to a gallon-size, airtight zip-top bag. Purées will last in the freezer for up to 6 months; they can be thawed in the refrigerator overnight or in the microwave on the defrost setting.

HERBS AND SPICES: Warm spices like cinnamon, nutmeg, ginger, coriander, and cumin pair really well with sweet potato.

PUMPKIN PURÉE

● ● ●

YIELD: 15 (1-OUNCE) FREEZER CUBES **PREP TIME:** 10 MINUTES **COOK TIME:** 10 TO 15 MINUTES

Pumpkin is one of my favorite fall and winter vegetables. It's also an excellent choice for your baby because it's slightly sweet and has a naturally smooth texture. It takes a bit of prep work (and time, if you choose to roast it), but the flavor is so worth it. Pumpkin is also a great source of fiber and vitamins A, C, and E.

FREEZER-FRIENDLY

DAIRY-FREE

GLUTEN-FREE

NUT-FREE

VEGAN

VEGETARIAN

1½ pounds pumpkin, peeled, seeded, pulp removed, and cut into 1-inch cubes (or 1 [16-ounce] package frozen pumpkin, thawed)

¼ cup water, plus more if needed

1. Pour about ½ inch of water into a medium pot and set a steamer basket inside it. Arrange the pumpkin evenly inside the basket. Bring the water to a simmer over medium heat and steam for 10 to 15 minutes, until the pumpkin is soft (cover the pot to speed up the cooking time).

2. Transfer the cooked pumpkin and steaming water to a blender.

3. Add a pinch of herb or spice (if using).

4. Blend until combined and very smooth. (Add more water as needed; start by adding a little bit at a time, since you can always add more.)

5. Transfer the purée to ice cube trays and freeze.

STORAGE: Freeze overnight, then transfer the frozen cubes to a gallon-size, airtight zip-top bag. Purées will last in the freezer for up to 6 months; they can be thawed in the refrigerator overnight or in the microwave on the defrost setting.

HERBS AND SPICES: Pumpkin goes perfectly with classic fall spices like ginger, cinnamon, nutmeg, allspice, cloves, and sage.

CAULIFLOWER PURÉE

• • •

YIELD: 15 (1-OUNCE) FREEZER CUBES   **PREP TIME:** 10 MINUTES   **COOK TIME:** 10 TO 15 MINUTES

Part of the cruciferous vegetable family, cauliflower is full of phytochemicals that are said to help prevent cancer. It is also packed with fiber, protein, and vitamins A and C. You can steam the cauliflower florets and stems together, since all of it is great for your baby. For a slightly different flavor, try roasting the cauliflower florets before puréeing them; this will bring out some of the vegetable's natural sugars and caramelize it a bit, too.

FREEZER-FRIENDLY

DAIRY-FREE

GLUTEN-FREE

NUT-FREE

VEGAN

VG

VEGETARIAN

1½ pounds cauliflower, cut into florets (or 1 [16-ounce] package frozen cauliflower, thawed)

¼ cup water, plus more if needed

1. Pour about ½ inch of water into a medium pot and set a steamer basket inside it. Arrange the cauliflower evenly inside the basket. Bring the water to a simmer over medium heat and steam for 10 to 15 minutes, until the cauliflower is soft (cover the pot to speed up the cooking time).

2. Transfer the cooked cauliflower and steaming water to a blender.

3. Add a pinch of herb or spice (if using).

4. Blend until combined and very smooth. (Add more water as needed; start by adding a little bit at a time, since you can always add more.)

5. Transfer the purée to ice cube trays and freeze.

STORAGE: Freeze overnight, then transfer the frozen cubes to a gallon-size, airtight zip-top bag. Purées will last in the freezer for up to 6 months; they can be thawed in the refrigerator overnight or in the microwave on the defrost setting.

HERBS AND SPICES: Cauliflower is a mild vegetable, so it will take on the flavor of any spice you combine it with. Some favorites are cumin, coriander, ginger, garlic, or paprika.

PEA PURÉE

• • •

YIELD: 15 (1-OUNCE) FREEZER CUBES   **PREP TIME:** 5 MINUTES   **COOK TIME:** 10 TO 15 MINUTES

Fresh peas are delicious. The only drawback is that they're available for only a few weeks in the spring. So I recommend using frozen peas for this purée, which also cuts out all the prep time. Layla didn't love pea purée by itself because of its strong flavor, but when mixed with carrots or a sweeter purée, she gobbled it right up. If summer flavor is what you're after, substitute the frozen peas with frozen sweet corn and prepare it the same way.

FREEZER-FRIENDLY

DAIRY-FREE

GLUTEN-FREE

NUT-FREE

V

VEGAN

VG

VEGETARIAN

1 (16-ounce) package frozen peas

¼ cup water, plus more if needed

1. Pour about ½ inch of water into a medium pot and set a steamer basket inside it. Arrange the peas evenly inside the basket. Bring the water to a simmer over medium heat and steam for 10 to 15 minutes until the peas are soft (cover the pot to speed up the cooking time).

2. Transfer the cooked peas and steaming water to a blender.

3. Add a pinch of herb or spice (if using).

4. Blend until combined and very smooth. (Add more water as needed; start by adding a little bit at a time, since you can always add more.)

5. Transfer the purée to ice cube trays and freeze.

STORAGE: Freeze overnight, then transfer the frozen cubes to a gallon-size, airtight zip-top bag. Purées will last in the freezer for up to 6 months; they can be thawed in the refrigerator overnight or in the microwave on the defrost setting.

HERBS AND SPICES: Peas and mint are my favorite pairing, but you can also try basil, grated lemon zest, or ground cumin.

SPINACH PURÉE

• • •

YIELD: 15 (1-OUNCE) FREEZER CUBES   **PREP TIME:** 5 MINUTES   **COOK TIME:** 10 TO 20 MINUTES

Spinach is a nutritional superstar, loaded with fiber and vitamins such as iron, folate, and vitamins A, C, E, and K. Spinach is wonderfully versatile because it takes on the flavor of whatever it is mixed with. So if your little one isn't a fan of it on its own, try mixing it with a fruit purée, a sweeter vegetable purée, or even plain whole-milk yogurt. This recipe will work with any dark leafy green, such as kale or Swiss chard. You can also substitute frozen spinach (1 [16-ounce] package, thawed). The same method applies, but no prep work is required.

FREEZER-
FRIENDLY

DAIRY-FREE

GLUTEN-FREE

NUT-FREE

VEGAN

VEGETARIAN

1½ pounds baby spinach leaves (or any dark, leafy greens, like kale or Swiss chard), chopped

¼ cup water, plus more if needed

1. Pour about ½ inch of water into a medium pot and set a steamer basket inside it. Arrange the spinach evenly inside the basket. Bring the water to a simmer over medium heat and steam for 10 to 20 minutes, until the spinach is soft (cover the pot to speed up the cooking time).

2. Transfer the cooked spinach and steaming water to a blender.

3. Add a pinch of herb or spice (if using).

4. Blend until combined and very smooth. (Add more water as needed; start by adding a little bit at a time, since you can always add more.)

5. Transfer the purée to ice cube trays and freeze.

STORAGE: Freeze overnight, then transfer the frozen cubes to a gallon-size, airtight zip-top bag. Purées will last in the freezer for up to 6 months; they can be thawed in the refrigerator overnight or in the microwave on the defrost setting.

HERBS AND SPICES: Spinach does well with strong herbs and spices, as do most dark, leafy greens. Season spinach with basil, dill, rosemary, garlic, ginger, nutmeg, allspice, cumin, or thyme.

BROCCOLI PURÉE

• • •

YIELD: 15 (1-OUNCE) FREEZER CUBES   **PREP TIME:** 10 MINUTES   **COOK TIME:** 10 TO 15 MINUTES

Like its cauliflower relative, broccoli is a nutritional powerhouse. This cruciferous vegetable is packed with vitamins C and K, fiber, and folate. Expose your child to this superfood early, and she'll be a fan for life. To this day, steamed broccoli remains one of Layla's favorite vegetable preparations.

FREEZER-
FRIENDLY

DAIRY-FREE

GLUTEN-FREE

NUT-FREE

V

VEGAN

VG

VEGETARIAN

1½ pounds broccoli, cut into florets (or 1 [16-ounce] package frozen broccoli, thawed)

¼ cup water, plus more if needed

1. Pour about ½ inch of water into a medium pot and set a steamer basket inside it. Arrange the broccoli evenly inside the basket. Bring the water to a simmer over medium heat and steam for 10 to 15 minutes, until the broccoli is soft (cover the pot to speed up the cooking time).

2. Transfer the cooked broccoli and steaming water to a blender.

3. Add a pinch of herb or spice (if using).

4. Blend until combined and very smooth. (Add more water as needed; start by adding a little bit at a time, since you can always add more.)

5. Transfer the purée to ice cube trays and freeze.

STORAGE: Freeze overnight, then transfer the frozen cubes to a gallon-size, airtight zip-top bag. Purées will last in the freezer for up to 6 months; they can be thawed in the refrigerator overnight or in the microwave on the defrost setting.

HERBS AND SPICES: Broccoli is delicious with garlic, oregano, rosemary, and thyme.

OATMEAL PURÉE

• • •

YIELD: 15 (1-OUNCE) FREEZER CUBES   **PREP TIME:** 5 MINUTES   **COOK TIME:** 10 MINUTES

Although baby oatmeal is sold at the market, it's actually super easy and much cheaper to make it yourself. Baby cereal is nothing more than finely ground grains, something you can accomplish without any trouble at home. Oatmeal is a great first cereal to offer your child, because it's full of fiber, vitamins, and minerals and mixes well with all fruit and veggie purées.

FREEZER-FRIENDLY

DAIRY-FREE

NUT-FREE

Ⓥ

VEGAN

ⓋⒼ

VEGETARIAN

½ cup rolled oats   **2 cups water**

1. In a food processor or blender, grind the oats to a fine powder.

2. In a small pot, bring the water to a simmer. Add the ground oats. Cook on low heat until the oats are soft, about 10 minutes. (This can also be done in the microwave, on high for 2 to 3 minutes.)

3. Transfer to ice cube trays and freeze.

STORAGE: Freeze overnight, then transfer the frozen cubes to a gallon-size, airtight zip-top bag. Purées will last in the freezer for up to 6 months; they can be thawed in the refrigerator overnight or in the microwave on the defrost setting.

HERBS AND SPICES: Oatmeal tastes wonderful with warm spices like cinnamon, nutmeg, and allspice. You can also try ground cardamom or saffron for a twist on traditional oatmeal!

BARLEY PURÉE

• • •

YIELD: 15 (1-OUNCE) FREEZER CUBES   **PREP TIME:** 5 MINUTES   **COOK TIME:** 10 MINUTES

Once you have offered your baby oatmeal, you can start branching out to other grains. Barley is one of my favorites for baby cereal, as it's high in fiber, manganese, selenium, and magnesium.

FREEZER-FRIENDLY

DAIRY-FREE

NUT-FREE

V

VEGAN

VG

VEGETARIAN

½ cup dried barley   **2 cups water**

1. In a food processor or blender, grind the barley to a fine powder.

2. In a small pot, bring the water to a simmer. Add the ground barley. Cook on low heat until the barley is soft, about 10 minutes. (This can also be done in the microwave, on high for 2 to 3 minutes.)

3. Transfer to ice cube trays and freeze.

STORAGE: Freeze overnight, then transfer the frozen cubes to a gallon-size, airtight zip-top bag. Purées will last in the freezer for up to 6 months; they can be thawed in the refrigerator overnight or in the microwave on the defrost setting.

HERBS AND SPICES: Barley purée has a similar flavor profile to oatmeal, so cinnamon and nutmeg are great additions. For a more savory cereal, try basil, chives, parsley, or dill.

LENTIL PURÉE

• • •

YIELD: 15 (1-OUNCE) FREEZER CUBES   **PREP TIME:** 5 MINUTES   **COOK TIME:** 1 HOUR

Lentils are extremely versatile, and babies love their mild flavor. Mix this purée with a fruit or vegetable purée if you're looking to add a little more sustenance to your baby's meal. As an added bonus, lentils are high in fiber, protein, folate, and iron.

FREEZER-FRIENDLY

DAIRY-FREE

GLUTEN-FREE

NUT-FREE

V

VEGAN

VG

VEGETARIAN

1 cup dried lentils (red, yellow, brown, or green)

2½ cups water, plus more if needed

1. Put the lentils and water in a large pot and bring to a boil.

2. Reduce to a simmer. Let cook for 1 hour or until the lentils are very soft.

3. Transfer the cooked lentils and remaining water to a blender.

4. Blend until combined and very smooth. (Add more water if all the water has been absorbed. Start by adding a little bit at a time, as you can always add more.)

5. Add a pinch of herb or spice (if using).

6. Transfer to ice cube trays and freeze.

STORAGE: Freeze overnight, then transfer the frozen cubes to a gallon-size, airtight zip-top bag. Purées will last in the freezer for up to 6 months; they can be thawed in the refrigerator overnight or in the microwave on the defrost setting.

HERBS AND SPICES: Lentils have such a mild flavor that you can season them with literally any spice. My favorites are cumin, coriander, turmeric, garam masala, curry powder, cardamom, and cilantro.

CHICKPEA PURÉE

• • •

YIELD: 15 (1-OUNCE) FREEZER CUBES   **PREP TIME:** 5 MINUTES   **COOK TIME:** 20 MINUTES

I like to call this recipe "baby hummus." If you add a bit of garlic and grated lemon zest, it will taste much like the hummus you buy at the store. Chickpeas are packed with protein and are high in zinc, folate, and iron.

FREEZER-FRIENDLY

DAIRY-FREE

GLUTEN-FREE

NUT-FREE

Ⓥ

VEGAN

VG

VEGETARIAN

2 cups water (or enough to cover the chickpeas)

2 (15-ounce) cans chickpeas, rinsed and drained

1. In a pot of water, boil the chickpeas for about 20 minutes, until soft.

2. Transfer the chickpeas to a blender, add about ½ cup of the boiling water and a pinch of herb or spice (if using), and purée.

3. Transfer to ice cube trays and freeze.

STORAGE: Freeze overnight, then transfer the frozen cubes to a gallon-size, airtight zip-top bag. Purées will last in the freezer for up to 6 months; they can be thawed in the refrigerator overnight or in the microwave on the defrost setting.

HERBS AND SPICES: The sky's the limit here. Some of my favorites include garlic, grated lemon zest, cumin, coriander, and cinnamon.

WHITE BEAN PURÉE

• • •

YIELD: 15 (1-OUNCE) FREEZER CUBES

PREP TIME: 5 MINUTES, PLUS 8 HOURS TO SOAK   **COOK TIME:** 2 HOURS

White beans are very mild and take on the flavor of anything you combine them with. This purée is an excellent way to add extra protein to any of the purées you offer your baby on a daily basis. Feel free to use any type of bean for this recipe. Black, pinto, kidney, and navy beans are all equally good options. If you don't have time to soak dried beans overnight, you can use canned beans, which also cuts down on the cooking time (see Tip).

FREEZER-
FRIENDLY

DAIRY-FREE

GLUTEN-FREE

NUT-FREE

VEGAN

VG

VEGETARIAN

2 cups water (or enough to cover the beans)

1 cup dried white beans, soaked overnight, rinsed and drained

1. In a pot of water, bring the beans to a boil, then reduce the heat and simmer until soft (about 2 hours).

2. Transfer the beans to a blender, add about ½ cup of the simmering water and a pinch of herb or spice (if using), and purée.

3. Transfer to ice cube trays and freeze.

TIP: To save time, use 2 (15-ounce) cans of white beans instead. Drain and rinse them, then boil the beans in a pot of water for about 20 minutes, until soft. Transfer the beans to a blender, add about ½ cup of the boiling water, and purée.

STORAGE: Freeze overnight, then transfer the frozen cubes to a gallon-size, airtight zip-top bag. Purées will last in the freezer for up to 6 months; they can be thawed in the refrigerator overnight or in the microwave on the defrost setting.

HERBS AND SPICES: Savory spices work really well with white beans. Some of my favorites include bay leaves, thyme, sage, oregano, and rosemary.

TOFU PURÉE

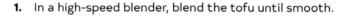

YIELD: 15 (1-OUNCE) FREEZER CUBES   **PREP TIME:** 5 MINUTES

Tofu is similar to avocado in that it can quickly be whipped up into an easy, no-cook purée. Tofu has a very mild flavor that adapts well to other flavors. I'd encourage you to add it to baby "smoothies" and fruit-vegetable purée combos as your baby gets older, since it's high in plant-based protein.

FREEZER-FRIENDLY

DAIRY-FREE

GLUTEN-FREE

NUT-FREE

V

VEGAN

VG

VEGETARIAN

1 (12- to 16-ounce) block silken tofu, drained

1. In a high-speed blender, blend the tofu until smooth.

2. Transfer to ice cube trays and freeze.

STORAGE: Freeze overnight, then transfer the frozen cubes to a gallon-size, airtight zip-top bag. Purées will last in the freezer for up to 6 months; they can be thawed in the refrigerator overnight or in the microwave on the defrost setting.

FISH PURÉE

● ● ●

Fish is a great source of protein for your little one. You can replace the cod in this recipe with any mild whitefish, like rainbow trout or haddock. In most cases, fishmongers have removed all the bones, but you'll still want to carefully pick through the fillet to ensure all the pinbones are gone before steaming.

**FREEZER-
FRIENDLY**

DAIRY-FREE

GLUTEN-FREE

NUT-FREE

1 cup water (or enough to cover the fish)

8 ounces cod or other fish, skin and bones removed, cut into 4 pieces

1. In a small saucepan, bring the water to a simmer. Add the cod.

2. Cover and simmer over medium heat until the fish is opaque, 5 to 10 minutes.

3. Remove the cod from the water and allow it to cool slightly, reserving the cooking liquid. Purée in a blender or food processor, adding some of the poaching water for your desired consistency and a pinch of herb or spice (if using).

STORAGE: Refrigerate for up to 3 days or freeze in ice cube trays for up to 3 months. Thaw in the refrigerator overnight or in the microwave on the defrost setting.

HERBS AND SPICES: If you are adding herbs for older babies, tarragon is a great choice here.

POULTRY PURÉE

● ● ●

YIELD: 4 (1-OUNCE) CUBES   **PREP TIME:** 5 MINUTES   **COOK TIME:** 5 TO 10 MINUTES

You can use any type of poultry, and if you like, use a combination of white and dark meat or just one or the other. Thin the purée as you make it, and then before you serve it to your baby, thin it further with a little water or even another fruit or vegetable purée.

FREEZER-
FRIENDLY

DAIRY-FREE

GLUTEN-FREE

NUT-FREE

1 cup water (or enough to cover the poultry)

8 ounces boneless, skinless chicken or turkey thigh or breast, cut into about 8 pieces

1. In a small saucepan, bring the water to a simmer. Add the chicken or turkey.

2. Cover and simmer over medium heat until the poultry is cooked and opaque, 5 to 10 minutes.

3. Remove the poultry from the water and allow it to cool slightly, reserving the cooking liquid. Purée in a blender or food processor, adding a little of the poaching water for your desired consistency.

TIP: If using dark meat, remove any strands of fat sticking to the meat before poaching it.

STORAGE: Refrigerate for up to 3 days or freeze in ice cube trays for up to 3 months. Thaw in the refrigerator overnight or in the microwave on the defrost setting.

BEEF PURÉE

• • •

YIELD: 4 (1-OUNCE) CUBES   **PREP TIME:** 5 MINUTES   **COOK TIME:** 10 MINUTES

Get your protein, B vitamins, iron, and zinc right here. While this is a beef purée, you can use any other red meat, such as lamb. Since you will be poaching it, it's helpful to choose a lean, relatively tender cut such as sirloin.

FREEZER-
FRIENDLY

DAIRY-FREE

GLUTEN-FREE

NUT-FREE

1 cup water (or enough to cover the beef)

8 ounces lean beef, cut into ½-inch cubes

1. In a small saucepan, bring the water to a simmer. Add the beef cubes.

2. Cover and simmer on medium heat until the beef is fully cooked and brown, about 10 minutes.

3. Remove the beef from the water and allow it to cool slightly, reserving the cooking liquid. Purée in a blender or food processor, adding a little of the poaching water for your desired consistency.

TIP: Trim away any separable fat from the cubes of beef before simmering them. Add enough water to cover the cubes completely by about ½ inch.

STORAGE: Refrigerate for up to 3 days or freeze in ice cube trays for up to 3 months. Thaw in the refrigerator overnight or in the microwave on the defrost setting.

PURÉE MIX-INS

My favorite part about making Layla's baby food was coming up with different spice and flavor combinations to mix into her purées. But mix-ins don't have to be limited to herbs and spices. There are lots of other enticing options you can add to your baby's meals to increase nutrients and add texture or flavor. Here are my favorite mix-ins, with some tips on how to use them:

- **Yogurt:** I added yogurt to a lot of my daughter's vegetable purées to make them more palatable (yogurt and green beans were an especially huge hit). I recommend plain full-fat yogurt, but you can also use plain full-fat Greek yogurt for a bit of a protein boost and a thicker purée. You can add anywhere from 1 teaspoon to 1 tablespoon yogurt to any of the purées in this chapter. Avoid flavored yogurts or "fruit-at-the-bottom" yogurts, as those are packed with sugar.

- **Seeds:** If you're thinking about adding seeds to your baby's purée, ground flaxseed and ground chia seeds are ideal. Loaded with healthy fats, fiber, and protein, they are an excellent addition to any of the fruit or veggie purées in this chapter.

- **Nuts:** Although your baby is too small to chew on whole nuts, nut butters and nut flour can be good add-ins for your baby's food. Peanut, almond, and cashew butters are the easiest to find, and they combine well with all fruit and grain purées as well as most veggie purées (broccoli with peanut and squash with almond are two delicious combinations). Since nuts are one of the Big 8 allergens, introduce only one nut at a time, watching for two days for any adverse reaction before starting another.

- **Cheese:** This is a great way to get some extra calcium, protein, and healthy fats into your baby's diet. Look for full-fat mild cheeses (e.g., Colby, Jack, Cheddar) and full-fat cottage cheese. You can add cottage cheese to any purée just as you would yogurt; mix in firm cheese by finely shredding it before adding it to a purée.

- **Meat and fish:** In the early days, limit meat and fish to small amounts thinned with fruit purée, vegetable purée, breast milk, or water. As your baby grows more accustomed to the texture, you can gradually thin them less. Your baby will indicate if your mixture is too thick. If she immediately pushes it out of her mouth, thin it a bit and try again.

- **Wheat germ:** I love wheat germ because it's packed with iron, vitamin B, folic acid, and vitamin E. It can be used as a mix-in to thicken any purée and make it a little heartier for your baby.

- **Oatmeal and ground grains:** Oatmeal and grains can be mixed with formula or breast milk to be served as baby

"cereal," but you can also use them to thicken any purée. I recommend grinding rolled oats, dried barley, or quinoa in a food processor to a fine powdery consistency (like flour) before cooking and then adding to a purée.

- **Herbs and spices:** These are some of my favorite mix-ins for baby food. A few great ones to try are garlic, basil, rosemary, dill, oregano, grated lemon zest, ginger, cinnamon, mint, nutmeg, curry powder (just make sure it's not too spicy), cumin, coriander, cardamom, turmeric, garam masala, and allspice.

Just add a pinch to your purées. Many of the recipes include their own suggestions for herbs or spices to add.

- **Coconut:** There are so many ways to use coconut in your baby food, from coconut milk to coconut oil. Try adding a little full-fat coconut milk to fruit purées, oatmeal or grain purées, or any of the squash purées. You can also add ½ teaspoon coconut oil to any purée for some healthy fats. Later, when your baby transitions to mini meals, consider using coconut oil for cooking as well.

Chapter Four

CREAMY COMBINATION PURÉES

6 TO 8 MONTHS

At this point, your baby is a single-ingredient purée champ. And now that you've mastered the purées in chapter 3, you are probably eager to start mixing and matching purées and spices for your little one. I offered Layla about 10 single-ingredient purées in the first month, and then, once I was sure she had no adverse reactions, I began mixing and matching those 10 purées along with new foods every few days.

Combining different purées is an easy way to get babies familiar with—and enjoying—a range of flavorful and nutritionally beneficial foods. Although you'll find lots of suggestions in this chapter, feel free to experiment based on your child's flavor preferences. Have some fun with this. It's a joy to watch your baby's palate develop and see her become a more adventurous eater.

WHAT'S ON THE TABLE
6 TO 8 MONTHS

HOW OFTEN: 2 or 3 meals per day

WHAT TO EAT: Creamy purées, more flavors, increasing in thickness

HOW MUCH: 1 to 2 tablespoons, or more if your baby wants more

FINGER FOODS: Very small cubes of cheese; soft, small pieces of steamed veggies

WHAT TO DRINK: Water; 24 to 40 ounces of breast milk or formula every day in between meals

BLUEBERRY AND APPLE PURÉE

• • •

YIELD: 2 (2-OUNCE) SERVINGS   **PREP TIME:** 5 MINUTES

Blueberries are delicious, but for a baby they can be a little tart, so the apple in this purée helps balance the sweetness. This purée is rich in fiber and antioxidants as well as vitamin C.

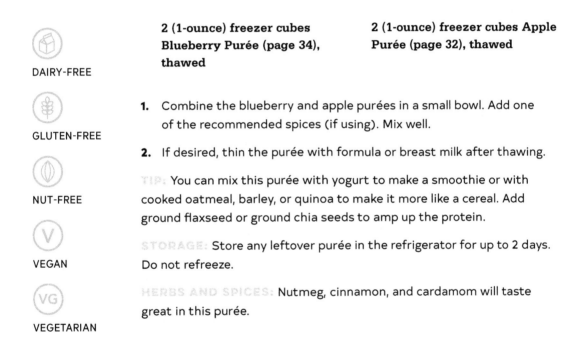

DAIRY-FREE

GLUTEN-FREE

NUT-FREE

VEGAN

VEGETARIAN

2 (1-ounce) freezer cubes Blueberry Purée (page 34), thawed

2 (1-ounce) freezer cubes Apple Purée (page 32), thawed

1. Combine the blueberry and apple purées in a small bowl. Add one of the recommended spices (if using). Mix well.

2. If desired, thin the purée with formula or breast milk after thawing.

TIP: You can mix this purée with yogurt to make a smoothie or with cooked oatmeal, barley, or quinoa to make it more like a cereal. Add ground flaxseed or ground chia seeds to amp up the protein.

STORAGE: Store any leftover purée in the refrigerator for up to 2 days. Do not refreeze.

HERBS AND SPICES: Nutmeg, cinnamon, and cardamom will taste great in this purée.

BANANA AND PEAR PURÉE

● ● ●

YIELD: 2 (2-OUNCE) SERVINGS   **PREP TIME:** 5 MINUTES

This is an all-time baby favorite—the natural sweetness of bananas and pears makes this a delicious purée that's perfect for breakfast. Mix this with some oatmeal, and you've got a balanced, satiating meal high in fiber, potassium, and vitamin C.

DAIRY-FREE

GLUTEN-FREE

NUT-FREE

V

VEGAN

VG

VEGETARIAN

3 (1-ounce) freezer cubes Pear Purée (page 37), thawed

1 (1-ounce) freezer cube Banana Purée (page 31), thawed

1. Combine the pear and banana purées in a small bowl. Add one of the recommended spices (if using). Mix well.

2. If desired, thin the purée with formula or breast milk after thawing.

TIP: You can mix this purée with yogurt to make a smoothie or with cooked oatmeal, barley, or quinoa to make it more like a cereal. Add ground flaxseed or ground chia seeds to amp up the protein.

STORAGE: Store any leftover purée in the refrigerator for up to 2 days. Do not refreeze.

HERBS AND SPICES: Warm spices, like cinnamon and nutmeg, pair well with this purée.

PRUNE AND APPLE PURÉE

• • •

YIELD: 2 (2-OUNCE) SERVINGS   **PREP TIME:** 5 MINUTES

This was my go-to purée for keeping Layla regular. The combination of fiber-rich prunes and apples make for a mild, sweet purée that has the added benefit of preventing constipation.

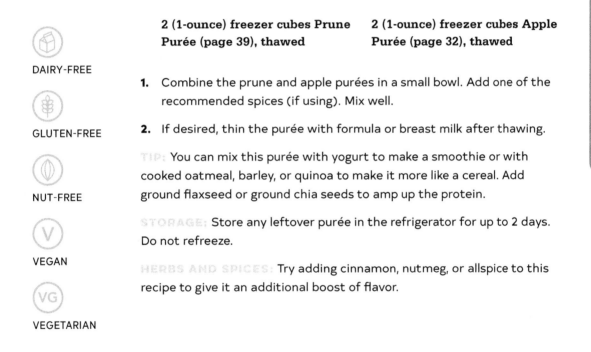

DAIRY-FREE

GLUTEN-FREE

NUT-FREE

VEGAN

VG

VEGETARIAN

2 (1-ounce) freezer cubes Prune Purée (page 39), thawed

2 (1-ounce) freezer cubes Apple Purée (page 32), thawed

1. Combine the prune and apple purées in a small bowl. Add one of the recommended spices (if using). Mix well.

2. If desired, thin the purée with formula or breast milk after thawing.

TIP: You can mix this purée with yogurt to make a smoothie or with cooked oatmeal, barley, or quinoa to make it more like a cereal. Add ground flaxseed or ground chia seeds to amp up the protein.

STORAGE: Store any leftover purée in the refrigerator for up to 2 days. Do not refreeze.

HERBS AND SPICES: Try adding cinnamon, nutmeg, or allspice to this recipe to give it an additional boost of flavor.

MANGO AND PEACH PURÉE

• • •

YIELD: 2 (2-OUNCE) SERVINGS   **PREP TIME:** 5 MINUTES

I like to call this a baby tropical-smoothie purée. Little ones will enjoy the sweetness of both fruits, and the recipe is bursting with vitamins A and C as well as folate. This is a good candidate for mixing with (or alternating with) a veggie purée if your baby is pickier about eating less-sweet vegetables.

DAIRY-FREE

GLUTEN-FREE

NUT-FREE

VEGAN

VEGETARIAN

2 (1-ounce) freezer cubes
Mango Purée (page 38), thawed

2 (1-ounce) freezer cubes Peach
Purée (page 36), thawed

1. Combine the mango and peach purées in a small bowl. Add one of the recommended spices (if using). Mix well.

2. If desired, thin the purée with formula or breast milk after thawing.

TIP: You can mix this purée with yogurt to make a smoothie or with cooked oatmeal, barley, or quinoa to make it more like a cereal. Add ground flaxseed or ground chia seeds to amp up the protein.

STORAGE: Store any leftover purée in the refrigerator for up to 2 days. Do not refreeze.

HERBS AND SPICES: Try cinnamon, allspice, or nutmeg with this purée. Savory herbs like mint and basil also taste great.

AVOCADO AND BANANA PURÉE

• • •

YIELD: 2 (2-OUNCE) SERVINGS   **PREP TIME:** 5 MINUTES

Avocados and bananas have a similar consistency, so they purée well together, and the banana adds a hint of sweetness to the rich avocado. This purée is high in potassium and vitamins C, E, and K. You can also add some apple purée to increase the fiber content.

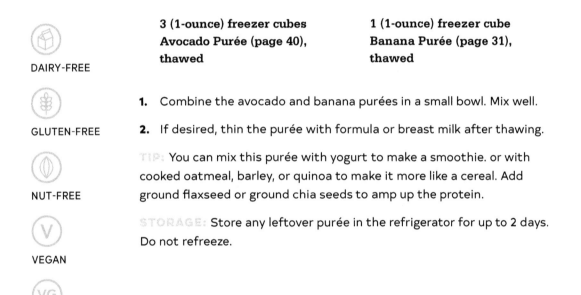

DAIRY-FREE

GLUTEN-FREE

NUT-FREE

V
VEGAN

VG
VEGETARIAN

3 (1-ounce) freezer cubes Avocado Purée (page 40), thawed

1 (1-ounce) freezer cube Banana Purée (page 31), thawed

1. Combine the avocado and banana purées in a small bowl. Mix well.

2. If desired, thin the purée with formula or breast milk after thawing.

TIP: You can mix this purée with yogurt to make a smoothie. or with cooked oatmeal, barley, or quinoa to make it more like a cereal. Add ground flaxseed or ground chia seeds to amp up the protein.

STORAGE: Store any leftover purée in the refrigerator for up to 2 days. Do not refreeze.

BEET, PEACH, AND APRICOT PURÉE

• • •

YIELD: 2 (2-OUNCE) SERVINGS   **PREP TIME:** 5 MINUTES

Available year-round, beets are one of the sweeter vegetables, which makes them perfect for pairing with fruit-forward purées. Peaches and apricots are abundant in the summer months, but you can just as easily use frozen peaches and other stone fruits. This purée is high in calcium, potassium, and vitamins A and C.

DAIRY-FREE

GLUTEN-FREE

NUT-FREE

VEGAN

VEGETARIAN

2 (1-ounce) freezer cubes Beet Purée (page 43), thawed

1 (1-ounce) freezer cube Peach Purée (page 36), thawed

1 (1-ounce) freezer cube Apricot Purée (page 35), thawed

1. Combine the beet, peach, and apricot purées in a small bowl. Add one of the recommended spices (if using). Mix well.

2. If desired, thin the purée with formula or breast milk after thawing.

TIP: You can mix this purée with yogurt to make a smoothie or with cooked oatmeal, barley, or quinoa to make it more like a cereal. Add ground flaxseed or ground chia seeds to amp up the protein.

STORAGE: Store any leftover purée in the refrigerator for up to 2 days. Do not refreeze.

HERBS AND SPICES: Try this purée with basil, sage, or thyme for some fresh, herbaceous flavors.

PUMPKIN, BANANA, AND CHIA SEED PURÉE

YIELD: 2 (2-OUNCE) SERVINGS **PREP TIME:** 5 MINUTES

Fall flavors come together in this purée, which reminds me of a healthy pumpkin pie. With a slightly sweet, nutty flavor, pumpkin is a great source of fiber and vitamins A, C, and E. When combined with potassium-rich bananas, this purée becomes both a nutritious and delicious choice for your little one.

6 TO 8 MONTHS

DAIRY-FREE

GLUTEN-FREE

NUT-FREE

VEGAN

VEGETARIAN

3 (1-ounce) freezer cubes
Pumpkin Purée (page 49),
thawed

1 (1-ounce) freezer cube
Banana Purée (page 31),
thawed

½ tablespoon ground
chia seeds

1. Combine the pumpkin and banana purées and the chia seeds in a small bowl. Add one of the recommended spices (if using). Mix well.

2. If desired, thin the purée with formula or breast milk after thawing.

TIP: You can mix this purée with yogurt to make a smoothie or with cooked oatmeal, barley, or quinoa to make it more like a cereal. Add ground flaxseed or more ground chia seeds to amp up the protein.

STORAGE: Store any leftover purée in the refrigerator for up to 2 days. Do not refreeze.

HERBS AND SPICES: Try this purée with ground ginger, cloves, allspice, nutmeg, or cinnamon for that trademark pumpkin pie flavor.

STRAWBERRY, RED BELL PEPPER, AND BEET PURÉE

• • •

YIELD: 2 (2-OUNCE) SERVINGS   **PREP TIME:** 5 MINUTES

While red bell peppers may seem like an unusual choice to combine with fruit, they are naturally sweet, so they work nicely in this purée. If you're looking to increase the sweetness, add a bit of apple purée.

DAIRY-FREE

GLUTEN-FREE

NUT-FREE

V

VEGAN

VG

VEGETARIAN

2 (1-ounce) freezer cubes strawberry purée (see Blueberry Purée, page 34), thawed

1 (1-ounce) freezer cube Red Bell Pepper Purée (page 42), thawed

1 (1-ounce) freezer cube Beet Purée (page 43), thawed

1. Combine the strawberry, red bell pepper, and beet purées in a small bowl. Add the lemon zest (if using). Mix well.

2. If desired, thin the purée with formula or breast milk after thawing.

TIP: You can mix this purée with yogurt to make a smoothie or with cooked oatmeal, barley, or quinoa to make it more like a cereal. Add ground flaxseed or ground chia seeds to amp up the protein.

STORAGE: Store any leftover purée in the refrigerator for up to 2 days. Do not refreeze.

HERBS AND SPICES: Try adding lemon zest for a fresh twist on this purée.

PEAR AND SPINACH PURÉE

• • •

YIELD: 2 (2-OUNCE) SERVINGS   **PREP TIME:** 5 MINUTES

This is like a baby green smoothie. The mild sweetness of the pears works well with spinach, which takes on the flavor of whatever it is paired with. Consider adding other fruit or veggie purées to make this even more of a nutritional powerhouse for your little one.

DAIRY-FREE

GLUTEN-FREE

NUT-FREE

V

VEGAN

VG

VEGETARIAN

2 (1-ounce) freezer cubes Pear Purée (page 37), thawed

2 (1-ounce) freezer cubes Spinach Purée (page 52), thawed

1. Combine the pear and spinach purées in a small bowl. Mix well.

2. If desired, thin the purée with formula or breast milk after thawing.

TIP: You can add yogurt to this purée to make a smoothie, or add cooked oatmeal, barley, or quinoa for more of a cereal. Add ground flaxseed or ground chia seeds to amp up the protein.

STORAGE: Store any leftover purée in the refrigerator for up to 2 days. Do not refreeze.

APPLE, SPINACH, AND AVOCADO PURÉE

• • •

YIELD: 2 (2-OUNCE) SERVINGS   **PREP TIME:** 5 MINUTES

Packed with fiber from the apples and spinach and healthy fats from the avocado, this creamy and mild purée is pleasing for little ones who are still adjusting to bolder flavors. Vitamins A, C, and K (along with folate, B vitamins, and iron) add to the benefits.

DAIRY-FREE

GLUTEN-FREE

NUT-FREE

VEGAN

VEGETARIAN

2 (1-ounce) freezer cubes Apple Purée (page 32), thawed

1 (1-ounce) freezer cube Spinach Purée (page 52), thawed

1 (1-ounce) freezer cube Avocado Purée (page 40), thawed

1. Combine the apple, spinach, and avocado purées in a small bowl. Mix well.

2. If desired, thin the purée with formula or breast milk after thawing.

TIP: You can mix this purée with yogurt to make a smoothie or with cooked oatmeal, barley, or quinoa to make it more like a cereal. Add ground flaxseed or ground chia seeds to amp up the protein.

STORAGE: Store any leftover purée in the refrigerator for up to 2 days. Do not refreeze.

ZUCCHINI AND BANANA PURÉE

• • •

YIELD: 2 (2-OUNCE) SERVINGS   **PREP TIME:** 5 MINUTES

Think of this purée as a healthy version of zucchini banana bread (especially if you add some baby oatmeal to it). Zucchini pairs well with both fruits and vegetables thanks to its light, delicate flavor. Banana adds a nice sweetness to this purée, plus a healthy dose of potassium.

DAIRY-FREE

GLUTEN-FREE

NUT-FREE

V
VEGAN

VG
VEGETARIAN

2 (1-ounce) freezer cubes
Zucchini Purée (page 44),
thawed

2 (1-ounce) freezer cubes
Banana Purée (page 31),
thawed

1. Combine the zucchini and banana purées in a small bowl. Add one of the recommended spices (if using). Mix well.

2. If desired, thin the purée with formula or breast milk after thawing.

TIP: If you'd like a slightly less sweet purée, use 3 cubes of zucchini and 1 cube of banana. You can mix this purée with yogurt to make a smoothie, or with cooked oatmeal, barley, or quinoa to make it more like a cereal. Add ground flaxseed or ground chia seeds to amp up the protein.

STORAGE: Store any leftover purée in the refrigerator for up to 2 days. Do not refreeze.

HERBS AND SPICES: Cardamom, cinnamon, allspice, and nutmeg are all fabulous with this purée.

ZUCCHINI, APPLE, CARROT, AND PEAR PURÉE

• • •

YIELD: 2 (2-OUNCE) SERVINGS   **PREP TIME:** 5 MINUTES

This combination purée was one of Layla's all-time favorites. Loaded with fiber, beta-carotene, folate, and vitamin C, this delicious and versatile recipe is pretty much guaranteed to please even the pickiest eaters.

DAIRY-FREE

GLUTEN-FREE

NUT-FREE

VEGAN

VG

VEGETARIAN

1 (1-ounce) freezer cube Zucchini Purée (page 44), thawed

1 (1-ounce) freezer cube Apple Purée (page 32), thawed

1 (1-ounce) freezer cube Carrot Purée (page 41), thawed

1 (1-ounce) freezer cube Pear Purée (page 37), thawed

1. Combine the zucchini, apple, carrot, and pear purées in a small bowl. Add one of the recommended spices (if using). Mix well.

2. If desired, thin the purée with formula or breast milk after thawing.

TIP: You can mix this purée with yogurt to make a smoothie or with cooked oatmeal, barley, or quinoa to make it more like a cereal. Add ground flaxseed or ground chia seeds to amp up the protein.

STORAGE: Store any leftover purée in the refrigerator for up to 2 days. Do not refreeze.

HERBS AND SPICES: Spices that pair well with this purée are those you'd use in a zucchini bread or muffin, like orange zest, cinnamon, and nutmeg.

PEACH, MANGO, AND CARROT PURÉE

• • •

YIELD: 2 (2-OUNCE) SERVINGS   **PREP TIME:** 5 MINUTES

This is a step up from the Mango and Peach Purée on page 72. Carrots give a rich earthiness to this purée, while mangos add luscious taste and tropical color. This yummy dish is a rich source of antioxidants, vitamin C, B vitamins, and folate.

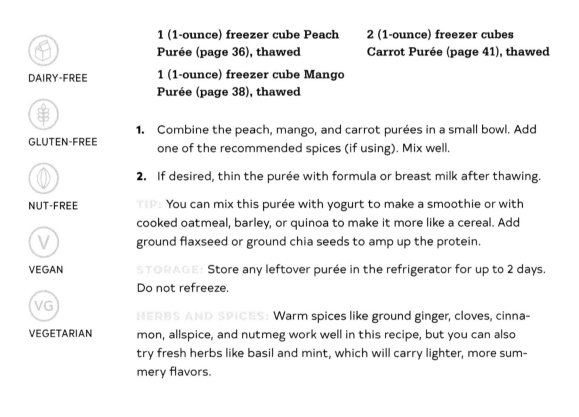

DAIRY-FREE

GLUTEN-FREE

NUT-FREE

V

VEGAN

VG

VEGETARIAN

1 (1-ounce) freezer cube Peach Purée (page 36), thawed

1 (1-ounce) freezer cube Mango Purée (page 38), thawed

2 (1-ounce) freezer cubes Carrot Purée (page 41), thawed

1. Combine the peach, mango, and carrot purées in a small bowl. Add one of the recommended spices (if using). Mix well.

2. If desired, thin the purée with formula or breast milk after thawing.

TIP: You can mix this purée with yogurt to make a smoothie or with cooked oatmeal, barley, or quinoa to make it more like a cereal. Add ground flaxseed or ground chia seeds to amp up the protein.

STORAGE: Store any leftover purée in the refrigerator for up to 2 days. Do not refreeze.

HERBS AND SPICES: Warm spices like ground ginger, cloves, cinnamon, allspice, and nutmeg work well in this recipe, but you can also try fresh herbs like basil and mint, which will carry lighter, more summery flavors.

PEAR, KALE, AND SPINACH PURÉE

• • •

YIELD: 2 (2-OUNCE) SERVINGS **PREP TIME:** 5 MINUTES

This purée is packed with superfood greens, which can sometimes have a slightly bitter taste; however, the addition of pear neutralizes some of those stronger flavors, creating a nicely balanced combination your little one is bound to love.

6 TO 8 MONTHS

DAIRY-FREE

GLUTEN-FREE

NUT-FREE

VEGAN

VG

VEGETARIAN

2 (1-ounce) freezer cubes Pear Purée (page 37), thawed

1 (1-ounce) freezer cube kale purée (see Spinach Purée page 52), thawed

1 (1-ounce) freezer cube Spinach Purée (page 52), thawed

1. Combine the pear, kale, and spinach purées in a small bowl. Mix well.

2. If desired, thin the purée with formula or breast milk after thawing.

TIP: You can mix this purée with yogurt to make a smoothie or with cooked oatmeal, barley, or quinoa to make it more like a cereal. Add ground flaxseed or ground chia seeds to amp up the protein.

STORAGE: Store any leftover purée in the refrigerator for up to 2 days. Do not refreeze.

THE SUPER EASY BABY FOOD COOKBOOK

CARROT AND BEET PURÉE

• • •

YIELD: 2 (2-OUNCE) SERVINGS   **PREP TIME:** 5 MINUTES

These two root vegetables are sweet, earthy, and abundant in the fall, making that a great time to offer this purée to your little one. It's also an excellent source of fiber, beta-carotene, and folate.

DAIRY-FREE

GLUTEN-FREE

NUT-FREE

VEGAN

VEGETARIAN

2 (1-ounce) freezer cubes Carrot Purée (page 41), thawed

2 (1-ounce) freezer cubes Beet Purée (page 43), thawed

1. Combine the carrot and beet purées in a small bowl. Add one of the recommended spices (if using). Mix well.

2. If desired, thin the purée with formula or breast milk after thawing.

TIP: To add protein to this purée, mix it with yogurt or cottage cheese. Always choose full-fat plain yogurt and cottage cheese for your little one. For regular cheese, choose mild, full-fat cheeses like Cheddar, mozzarella, or Jack. Adding cooked oatmeal, barley, or quinoa will thicken it and make it heartier. You may also mix in puréed lentils, beans, or chickpeas to add non-animal protein.

STORAGE: Store any leftover purée in the refrigerator for up to 2 days. Do not refreeze.

HERBS AND SPICES: This purée pairs well with spicy, fragrant, and warm herbs. Try cloves, coriander, cumin, ginger, fennel, allspice, or sage.

LENTIL AND CHICKPEA PURÉE

• • •

YIELD: 2 (2-OUNCE) SERVINGS   **PREP TIME:** 5 MINUTES

Packed with plant-based protein, this purée is delicious on its own, thanks to the mild flavor of the lentils and chickpeas, but it also pairs beautifully with any veggie purée and spices.

6 TO 8 MONTHS

DAIRY-FREE

GLUTEN-FREE

NUT-FREE

(V) VEGAN

(VG) VEGETARIAN

2 (1-ounce) freezer cubes Lentil Purée (page 57), thawed

2 (1-ounce) freezer cubes Chickpea Purée (page 58), thawed

1. Combine the lentil and chickpea purées in a small bowl. Add one of the recommended spices (if using). Mix well.

2. If desired, thin the purée with formula or breast milk after thawing.

TIP: To add protein to this purée, mix it with 1 to 2 tablespoons full-fat yogurt or cottage cheese or full-fat mild cheese like Cheddar, mozzarella, or Jack. You can also add 1 to 2 tablespoons cooked oatmeal, barley, or quinoa to thicken it and make it heartier. Mixing in 1 to 2 tablespoons of puréed meat will add protein, as well.

STORAGE: Store any leftover purée in the refrigerator for up to 2 days. Do not refreeze.

HERBS AND SPICES: Lentils and chickpeas pair especially well with fragrant spices like cumin, coriander, turmeric, and garam masala. You can even add a pinch of curry powder to this recipe—just make sure your curry powder doesn't have pepper or cayenne in it.

SWEET POTATO AND PUMPKIN PURÉE

• • •

YIELD: 2 (2-OUNCE) SERVINGS **PREP TIME:** 5 MINUTES

This recipe is the epitome of fall. The starchy texture and sweet, nutty taste of these vegetables pair seamlessly together, and they are rich in fiber, beta-carotene, and vitamin C to boot.

DAIRY-FREE

GLUTEN-FREE

NUT-FREE

VEGAN

VG
VEGETARIAN

2 (1-ounce) freezer cubes Sweet Potato Purée (page 48), thawed

2 (1-ounce) freezer cubes Pumpkin Purée (page 49), thawed

1. Combine the sweet potato and pumpkin purées in a small bowl. Add one of the recommended spices (if using). Mix well.

2. If desired, thin the purée with formula or breast milk after thawing.

TIP: To add protein to this purée, mix it with 1 to 2 tablespoons full-fat yogurt or cottage cheese or full-fat mild cheese like Cheddar, mozzarella, or Jack. You can also add 1 to 2 tablespoons cooked oatmeal, barley, or quinoa to thicken it and make it heartier. Mixing in 1 to 2 tablespoons of puréed meat will add protein, as well.

STORAGE: Store any leftover purée in the refrigerator for up to 2 days. Do not refreeze.

HERBS AND SPICES: Pumpkin pie spices, like cardamom, nutmeg, allspice, cloves, and cinnamon, are perfect with this purée. Try them one at a time first, then combine them all together for your little one.

BUTTERNUT SQUASH AND ZUCCHINI PURÉE

• • •

YIELD: 2 (2-OUNCE) SERVINGS **PREP TIME:** 5 MINUTES

Butternut squash goes well with just about any vegetable; here it's paired with zucchini for a sweet and savory purée. The zucchini cuts the sweetness of the butternut squash, and the combination is a great source of vitamins C, B$_6$, and E, plus potassium.

2 (1-ounce) freezer cubes Butternut Squash Purée (page 47), thawed

2 (1-ounce) freezer cubes Zucchini Purée (page 44), thawed

1. Combine the butternut squash and zucchini purées in a small bowl. Add one of the recommended spices (if using). Mix well.

2. If desired, thin the purée with formula or breast milk after thawing.

TIP: To add protein to this purée, mix it with 1 to 2 tablespoons full-fat yogurt or cottage cheese or full-fat mild cheese like Cheddar, mozzarella, or Jack. You can also add 1 to 2 tablespoons cooked oatmeal, barley, or quinoa to thicken it and make it heartier. Mixing in 1 to 2 tablespoons of puréed meat will add protein, as well.

STORAGE: Store any leftover purée in the refrigerator for up to 2 days. Do not refreeze.

HERBS AND SPICES: Try sweet spices like coriander, ginger, or allspice, or more savory herbs like oregano, thyme, or rosemary. Both pair beautifully with the squashes.

DAIRY-FREE

GLUTEN-FREE

NUT-FREE

VEGAN

VEGETARIAN

6 TO 8 MONTHS

SWEET CORN AND YELLOW SQUASH PURÉE

● ● ●

YIELD: 2 (2-OUNCE) SERVINGS   **PREP TIME:** 5 MINUTES

It's summer in a bowl! Sweet yellow corn tastes best in the late spring and summer months, as does summer squash (this recipe calls for yellow squash but any summer squash will do). Both of these veggies have a mild, sweet flavor and are rich in vitamin C.

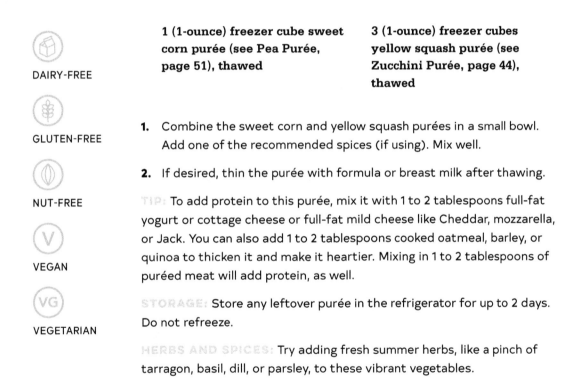

DAIRY-FREE

GLUTEN-FREE

NUT-FREE

V

VEGAN

VG

VEGETARIAN

1 (1-ounce) freezer cube sweet corn purée (see Pea Purée, page 51), thawed

3 (1-ounce) freezer cubes yellow squash purée (see Zucchini Purée, page 44), thawed

1. Combine the sweet corn and yellow squash purées in a small bowl. Add one of the recommended spices (if using). Mix well.

2. If desired, thin the purée with formula or breast milk after thawing.

TIP: To add protein to this purée, mix it with 1 to 2 tablespoons full-fat yogurt or cottage cheese or full-fat mild cheese like Cheddar, mozzarella, or Jack. You can also add 1 to 2 tablespoons cooked oatmeal, barley, or quinoa to thicken it and make it heartier. Mixing in 1 to 2 tablespoons of puréed meat will add protein, as well.

STORAGE: Store any leftover purée in the refrigerator for up to 2 days. Do not refreeze.

HERBS AND SPICES: Try adding fresh summer herbs, like a pinch of tarragon, basil, dill, or parsley, to these vibrant vegetables.

CAULIFLOWER AND SWEET POTATO PURÉE

• • •

YIELD: 2 (2-OUNCE) SERVINGS   **PREP TIME:** 5 MINUTES

Think of this recipe as a healthier version of baby mashed potatoes. White potatoes are replaced with sweet potatoes, which are higher in vitamins, fiber, and other nutrients, and cauliflower adds an antioxidant punch.

DAIRY-FREE

GLUTEN-FREE

NUT-FREE

V
VEGAN

VG
VEGETARIAN

2 (1-ounce) freezer cubes Cauliflower Purée (page 50), thawed

2 (1-ounce) freezer cubes Sweet Potato Purée (page 48), thawed

1. Combine the cauliflower and sweet potato purées in a small bowl. Add one of the recommended spices (if using). Mix well.

2. If desired, thin the purée with formula or breast milk after thawing.

TIP: To add protein to this purée, mix it with 1 to 2 tablespoons full-fat yogurt or cottage cheese or full-fat mild cheese like Cheddar, mozzarella, or Jack. You can also add 1 to 2 tablespoons cooked oatmeal, barley, or quinoa to thicken it and make it heartier. Mixing in 1 to 2 tablespoons of puréed meat will add protein, as well.

STORAGE: Store any leftover purée in the refrigerator for up to 2 days. Do not refreeze.

HERBS AND SPICES: A pinch of garlic powder tastes great in this purée, but so do spices like cumin, coriander, turmeric, and nutmeg, which all pair well with both veggies.

ZUCCHINI AND RED BELL PEPPER PURÉE

• • •

YIELD: 2 (2-OUNCE) SERVINGS   **PREP TIME:** 5 MINUTES

The sweet tang of red bell peppers complements the light and mild flavor of zucchini in this purée. Bell peppers are an excellent source of vitamins A, C, and B$_6$, as well as folate and fiber. For older babies, I like to turn this purée into a "pasta sauce" by combining it with Italian herbs and whole-wheat pasta.

DAIRY-FREE

GLUTEN-FREE

NUT-FREE

V
VEGAN

VG
VEGETARIAN

2 (1-ounce) freezer cubes Zucchini Purée (page 44), thawed

2 (1-ounce) freezer cubes Red Bell Pepper Purée (page 42), thawed

1. Combine the zucchini and red bell pepper purées in a small bowl. Add one of the recommended spices (if using). Mix well.

2. If desired, thin the purée with formula or breast milk after thawing.

TIP: To add protein to this purée, mix it with 1 to 2 tablespoons full-fat yogurt or cottage cheese or full-fat mild cheese like Cheddar, mozzarella, or Jack. You can also add 1 to 2 tablespoons cooked oatmeal, barley, or quinoa to thicken it and make it heartier. Mixing in 1 to 2 tablespoons of puréed meat will add protein, as well.

STORAGE: Store any leftover purée in the refrigerator for up to 2 days. Do not refreeze.

HERBS AND SPICES: Garlic and Italian herbs like oregano, basil, rosemary, and thyme are delicious with this purée.

SPINACH, BROCCOLI, AND CAULIFLOWER PURÉE

• • •

YIELD: 2 (2-OUNCE) SERVINGS   **PREP TIME:** 5 MINUTES

This purée will fill your baby's tummy with healthy, high-fiber, antioxidant-rich veggies—perfect for growing bodies. If the flavor is a bit too strong for your little one, try mixing in some yogurt to cut some of the bitterness.

DAIRY-FREE

GLUTEN-FREE

NUT-FREE

(V)

VEGAN

(VG)

VEGETARIAN

1 (1-ounce) freezer cube Spinach Purée (page 52), thawed

1 (1-ounce) freezer cube Broccoli Purée (page 54), thawed

2 (1-ounce) freezer cubes Cauliflower Purée (page 50), thawed

1. Combine the spinach, broccoli, and cauliflower purées in a small bowl. Add one of the recommended spices (if using). Mix well.

2. If desired, thin the purée with formula or breast milk after thawing.

TIP: To add protein to this purée, mix it with 1 to 2 tablespoons full-fat yogurt or cottage cheese or full-fat mild cheese like Cheddar, mozzarella, or Jack. You can also add 1 to 2 tablespoons cooked oatmeal, barley, or quinoa to thicken it and make it heartier. Mixing in 1 to 2 tablespoons of puréed meat will add protein, as well.

STORAGE: Store any leftover purée in the refrigerator for up to 2 days. Do not refreeze.

HERBS AND SPICES: Cumin, coriander, and garlic are my favorites to add to this recipe.

SPINACH, PEA, AND PEAR PURÉE

• • •

YIELD: 2 (2-OUNCE) SERVINGS   **PREP TIME:** 5 MINUTES

Layla wasn't a huge fan of peas on their own, but she loved them when I mixed them with pear or another sweet fruit. Spinach is mild enough that it takes on the flavor of these other two ingredients, creating a combination purée that's packed with fiber, folate, and iron. Feel free to substitute Apple Purée (page 32) in place of the pear.

DAIRY-FREE

GLUTEN-FREE

NUT-FREE

(V)
VEGAN

(VG)
VEGETARIAN

1 (1-ounce) freezer cube Spinach Purée (page 52), thawed

1 (1-ounce) freezer cube Pea Purée (page 51), thawed

2 (1-ounce) freezer cubes Pear Purée (page 37), thawed

1. Combine the spinach, pea, and pear purées in a small bowl. Mix well.

2. If desired, thin the purée with formula or breast milk after thawing.

TIP: To add protein to this purée, you can mix it with 1 to 2 tablespoons full-fat yogurt or cottage cheese or full-fat mild cheese like Cheddar, mozzarella, or Jack. You can also add 1 to 2 tablespoons cooked oatmeal, barley, or quinoa to thicken it and make it heartier. Mixing in 1 to 2 tablespoons of puréed meat will add protein, as well.

STORAGE: Store any leftover purée in the refrigerator for up to 2 days. Do not refreeze.

CARROT, SPINACH, AND GREEN BEAN PURÉE

• • •

YIELD: 2 (2-OUNCE) SERVINGS   **PREP TIME:** 5 MINUTES

Green beans and carrots are a favorite on our Thanksgiving table, so why not let baby join the celebration? Regardless, this purée can be enjoyed year-round. Substitute Sweet Potato Purée (page 48) for the carrots for a delicious variation.

6 TO 8 MONTHS

DAIRY-FREE

GLUTEN-FREE

NUT-FREE

V

VEGAN

VG

VEGETARIAN

2 (1-ounce) freezer cubes Carrot Purée (page 41), thawed

1 (1-ounce) freezer cube Spinach Purée (page 52), thawed

1 (1-ounce) freezer cube Green Bean Purée (page 45), thawed

1. Combine the carrot, spinach, and green bean purées in a small bowl. Add one of the recommended spices (if using). Mix well.

2. If desired, thin the purée with formula or breast milk after thawing.

TIP: To add protein to this purée, mix it with 1 to 2 tablespoons full-fat yogurt or cottage cheese or full-fat mild cheese like Cheddar, mozzarella, or Jack. You can also add 1 to 2 tablespoons cooked oatmeal, barley, or quinoa to thicken it and make it heartier. Mixing in 1 to 2 tablespoons of puréed meat will add protein, as well.

STORAGE: Store any leftover purée in the refrigerator for up to 2 days. Do not refreeze.

HERBS AND SPICES: Grated orange zest and ground nutmeg will taste amazing in this recipe, or you can try a pinch of cumin, coriander, and turmeric to make these veggies pop.

BUTTERNUT SQUASH, BLACK BEAN, AND CARROT PURÉE

• • •

YIELD: 2 (2-OUNCE) SERVINGS   **PREP TIME:** 5 MINUTES

Think of this as a "baby burrito bowl." A great source of fiber and protein, this purée is also packed with beta-carotene and other vitamins and minerals. To make it even heartier, add some puréed avocado, brown rice cereal, and cheese.

DAIRY-FREE

GLUTEN-FREE

NUT-FREE

(V)

VEGAN

(VG)

VEGETARIAN

1 (1-ounce) freezer cube Butternut Squash Purée (page 47), thawed

2 (1-ounce) freezer cubes black bean purée (see White Bean Purée, page 59), thawed

1 (1-ounce) freezer cube Carrot Purée (page 41), thawed

1. Combine the butternut squash, black bean, and carrot purées in a small bowl. Add the cumin (if using). Mix well.

2. If desired, thin the purée with formula or breast milk after thawing.

TIP: To add protein to this purée, mix it with 1 to 2 tablespoons full-fat yogurt or cottage cheese or full-fat mild cheese like Cheddar, mozzarella, or Jack. You can also add 1 to 2 tablespoons cooked oatmeal, barley, or quinoa to thicken it and make it heartier. Mixing in 1 to 2 tablespoons of puréed meat will add protein, as well.

STORAGE: Store any leftover purée in the refrigerator for up to 2 days. Do not refreeze.

HERBS AND SPICES: A pinch of cumin takes this recipe to new heights.

YELLOW BELL PEPPER, NAVY BEAN, AND YELLOW SQUASH PURÉE

•••

YIELD: 2 (2-OUNCE) SERVINGS   **PREP TIME:** 5 MINUTES

Yellow veggies and protein-rich beans come together in this mild, slightly sweet purée. Mediterranean spices complement this recipe nicely, but babies will love it plain as well.

DAIRY-FREE

GLUTEN-FREE

NUT-FREE

VEGAN

VG VEGETARIAN

1 (1-ounce) freezer cube yellow bell pepper purée (see Red Bell Pepper Purée, page 42), thawed

2 (1-ounce) freezer cubes navy bean purée (see White Bean Purée, page 59), thawed

1 (1-ounce) freezer cube yellow squash purée (see Zucchini Purée, page 44), thawed

1. Combine the yellow bell pepper, navy bean, and yellow squash purées in a small bowl. Add one of the recommended spices (if using). Mix well.

2. If desired, thin the purée with formula or breast milk after thawing.

TIP: To add protein to this purée, mix it with 1 to 2 tablespoons full-fat yogurt or cottage cheese or full-fat mild cheese like Cheddar, mozzarella, or Jack. You can also add 1 to 2 tablespoons cooked oatmeal, barley, or quinoa to thicken it and make it heartier. Mixing in 1 to 2 tablespoons of puréed meat will add protein, as well.

STORAGE: Store any leftover purée in the refrigerator for up to 2 days. Do not refreeze.

HERBS AND SPICES: Try oregano, basil, rosemary, and garlic to give your little one an early taste of the Mediterranean.

BROCCOLI, CAULIFLOWER, CARROT, AND CHICKPEA PURÉE

● ● ●

YIELD: 2 (2-OUNCE) SERVINGS **PREP TIME:** 5 MINUTES

This is a true superfood purée combination, thanks to the antioxidants and minerals in the broccoli and cauliflower, protein in the chickpeas, beta-carotene in the carrots, and fiber in everything.

DAIRY-FREE

GLUTEN-FREE

NUT-FREE

VEGAN

VG

VEGETARIAN

1 (1-ounce) freezer cube Broccoli Purée (page 54), thawed

1 (1-ounce) freezer cube Cauliflower Purée (page 50), thawed

1 (1-ounce) freezer cube Carrot Purée (page 41), thawed

1 (1-ounce) freezer cube Chickpea Purée (page 58), thawed

1. Combine the broccoli, cauliflower, carrot, and chickpea purées in a small bowl. Add one of the recommended spices (if using). Mix well.

2. If desired, thin the purée with formula or breast milk after thawing.

TIP: To add protein to this purée, mix it with 1 to 2 tablespoons full-fat yogurt or cottage cheese or full-fat mild cheese like Cheddar, mozzarella, or Jack. You can also add 1 to 2 tablespoons cooked oatmeal, barley, or quinoa to thicken it and make it heartier. Mixing in 1 to 2 tablespoons of puréed meat will add protein, as well.

STORAGE: Store any leftover purée in the refrigerator for up to 2 days. Do not refreeze.

HERBS AND SPICES: Cumin, coriander, turmeric, or garam masala taste delicious in this recipe. If you're feeling adventurous, try adding a tiny pinch of each to this purée along with 1 tablespoon of cooked brown rice or quinoa cereal before serving it.

COD, BUTTERNUT SQUASH, AND APPLE PURÉE

• • •

YIELD: 2 (2½-OUNCE) SERVINGS   **PREP TIME:** 10 MINUTES

If you can't find cod, look for any whitefish that is locally available. You can even substitute salmon or trout if you wish, although the texture and flavor will be slightly different.

DAIRY-FREE

GLUTEN-FREE

NUT-FREE

1 (1-ounce) freezer cube cod purée (see Fish Purée, page 61), thawed

2 (1-ounce) freezer cubes Butternut Squash Purée (page 47), thawed

2 (1-ounce) freezer cubes Apple Purée (page 32), thawed

⅛ teaspoon ground cinnamon

1. In a small bowl, combine the cod, butternut squash, and apple purées and the cinnamon. Mix well.

2. Thin with a little breast milk, formula, or water to achieve the desired consistency.

STORAGE: Store any leftover purée in the refrigerator for up to 2 days. Do not refreeze.

TURKEY AND PUMPKIN PURÉE

• • •

YIELD: 2 (2-OUNCE) SERVINGS **PREP TIME:** 5 MINUTES

Doesn't this sound cozy for a baby's winter meal? This purée is a good source of protein, B vitamins, and vitamin A, and the addition of nutmeg adds a hint of sweetness. Feel free to substitute the turkey purée with chicken.

GLUTEN-FREE

NUT-FREE

2 (1-ounce) freezer cubes turkey purée (see Poultry Purée, page 62), thawed

2 (1-ounce) freezer cubes Pumpkin Purée (page 49), thawed

1 to 2 tablespoons plain whole-milk yogurt

Pinch ground nutmeg

1. Combine the turkey and pumpkin purées in a small bowl with the yogurt. Add the nutmeg. Mix well.

2. Thin the purée with formula or breast milk after thawing, if desired.

STORAGE: Store any leftover purée in the refrigerator for up to 2 days. Do not refreeze.

HERBS AND SPICES: Cinnamon is a great replacement spice here, as is allspice. A one-fingered pinch is all you need, or about one shake from a shaker.

BEEF, BARLEY, AND GREEN BEAN PURÉE

• • •

YIELD: 2 (3½-OUNCE) SERVINGS   **PREP TIME:** 5 MINUTES

This combination adds up to a full meal with all the trimmings. If you feel gluten is an issue, you can replace the barley with quinoa or gluten-free oats prepared with breast milk, formula, or water.

DAIRY-FREE

NUT-FREE

2 (1-ounce) freezer cubes Beef Purée (page 63), thawed

2 (1-ounce) freezer cubes Green Bean Purée (page 45), thawed

3 (1-ounce) freezer cubes Barley Purée (page 56), thawed

1. Combine the beef, green bean, and barley purées in a small bowl. Add a pinch of thyme (if using). Mix well.

2. If desired, thin the purée with formula or breast milk after thawing.

STORAGE: Store any leftover purée in the refrigerator for up to 2 days. Do not refreeze.

HERBS AND SPICES: Try thyme in this recipe. Dried thyme is stronger in flavor than fresh thyme, so add a smaller pinch if using dried. For fresh thyme, make sure it is chopped into very small pieces.

PURÉE MIX-AND-MATCH CHART

	Avocado	Apple	Prune	Peach	Pear	Mango	Banana	Apricot	Blueberry, Other Berry	Carrot	Butternut Squash, Pumpkin, Sweet Potato	Zucchini, Summer Squash	Green Beans	Cauliflower	Broccoli	Peas	Spinach, Dark Leafy Greens	Beet	Oatmeal, Barley, Quinoa	Chickpea, Lentil, White Bean, Legumes
Avocado		X		X	X	X	X		X	X	X		X	X	X	X		X		X
Apple	X		X	X	X	X	X	X	X	X	X	X	X	X	X	X	X	X	X	X
Prune		X		X	X	X	X				X								X	
Peach	X	X	X		X	X	X	X	X	X	X	X	X	X				X	X	
Pear	X	X	X	X			X	X	X	X	X	X	X	X	X	X		X	X	X
Mango	X	X	X	X			X	X	X	X	X		X	X	X	X	X	X	X	
Banana	X	X	X	X	X	X		X	X	X	X						X	X	X	X
Apricot		X		X	X	X	X		X	X	X		X				X	X	X	
Blueberry, Other Berry	X	X		X	X	X	X	X									X	X	X	
Carrot	X	X		X	X	X	X	X			X	X	X	X	X	X	X	X	X	X
Butternut Squash, Pumpkin, Sweet Potato	X	X	X	X	X	X	X	X		X		X	X	X	X	X	X	X	X	X

	Avocado	Apple	Prune	Peach	Pear	Mango	Banana	Apricot	Blueberry Other Berry	Carrot	Butternut Squash Pumpkin Sweet Potato	Zucchini Summer Squash	Green Beans	Cauliflower	Broccoli	Peas	Spinach Dark Leafy Greens	Beet	Oatmeal Barley Quinoa	Chickpea Lentil White Bean Legumes
Zucchini, Summer Squash		X		X	X	X				X	X		X	X	X		X		X	X
Green Beans	X	X		X	X	X		X		X	X	X		X	X		X		X	X
Cauliflower		X			X					X	X	X	X		X	X	X	X	X	X
Broccoli	X	X			X	X				X	X	X	X	X			X		X	X
Peas	X	X			X	X		X		X	X			X					X	X
Spinach, Dark Leafy Greens	X	X			X	X	X	X	X	X	X	X	X	X	X			X	X	X
Beet		X		X	X	X	X		X	X	X			X					X	X
Oatmeal, Barley, Quinoa	X	X	X	X	X	X	X	X	X	X	X	X	X	X	X	X	X	X		X
Chickpea, Lentil, White Bean, Legumes	X	X			X		X			X	X	X	X	X	X	X	X	X	X	

Nut Butter and Banana
Stackers, page 124

Chapter Five

HEARTY TEXTURES AND FINGER FOODS

9 TO 12 MONTHS

Once your baby has been on purées for some time and is comfortable with eating thicker combinations, you can start to make chunkier purées and soft finger foods. You'll probably want to continue to feed your child purées with a spoon (mostly to ensure that the food is actually going in your baby's mouth, and not all over his face), but this is a good time to offer him finger foods that he can pick up and attempt to eat on his own. Finger foods are great for teaching your baby how to chew and swallow, and they also allow your baby to practice dexterity—picking up individual cubes of food and putting them in his mouth is no easy feat for a little one. The recipes in this chapter start out with chunky combination purées and move on to soft finger foods. As your baby gets used to chunkier textures, you can begin to phase out the purées and incorporate a full rotation of regular soft foods.

HOW OFTEN: **3 meals per day**

WHAT TO EAT: **Chunky purées and soft foods**

HOW MUCH: **2 ounces of food**

FINGER FOODS: **Small bits of steamed veggies; well-cooked lentils or beans; small pieces of soft, raw fruits like avocado or banana; small bits of cooked pasta; little cubes of cheese**

WHAT TO DRINK: **Water; 24 to 40 ounces of breast milk or formula every day in between meals**

BABY RATATOUILLE

• • •

YIELD: 8 (2-OUNCE) SERVINGS   **PREP TIME:** 10 MINUTES   **COOK TIME:** 5 TO 10 MINUTES

Summer squashes like zucchini and yellow squash are delicious and flavorful, especially when mixed with herbs. The smooth texture of the red bell pepper purée and crushed tomatoes pairs well with the chunkier squash cubes. As your baby gets older, you can forgo the purées altogether and just serve all the veggies soft, much like a traditional ratatouille.

DAIRY-FREE

GLUTEN-FREE

NUT-FREE

VEGAN

VEGETARIAN

½ medium zucchini, cut into ¼-inch cubes

½ medium yellow squash, such as crookneck, cut into ¼-inch cubes

4 (1-ounce) freezer cubes Red Bell Pepper Purée (page 42), thawed

½ teaspoon dried Italian seasoning

¼ cup fresh or canned crushed tomatoes

1. Pour about ½ inch of water into a medium pot, and set a steamer basket inside it. Add the zucchini and yellow squash and bring the water to a simmer over medium heat. Steam for 5 to 10 minutes, until the zucchini and yellow squash are soft.

2. Transfer the zucchini and squash to a medium bowl and mash. Add the red bell pepper purée, Italian seasoning, and crushed tomatoes with their juices. Stir to combine.

3. Cool slightly before serving.

TIP: Feel free to experiment with fresh herbs in this recipe. Fresh basil, oregano, rosemary, and thyme will all work nicely and can replace the dried Italian seasoning. Shredded mozzarella and Parmesan cheese are also fun add-ins to this recipe.

STORAGE: Store any leftover ratatouille in the refrigerator for up to 3 days.

SOUTHWEST BLACK BEAN SOUP

• • •

YIELD: 8 (2-OUNCE) SERVINGS **PREP TIME:** 10 MINUTES **COOK TIME:** 10 MINUTES

One of Layla's favorite meals is black beans, corn, brown rice, peppers, and avocado. I call it black bean "soup" since the purée makes it thin, but as your child gets older, you can leave it chunky and offer it more like a burrito bowl.

DAIRY-FREE

GLUTEN-FREE

NUT-FREE

VEGAN

VEGETARIAN

1 cup canned black beans, rinsed and drained

1 garlic clove, minced

½ teaspoon ground cumin

4 (1-ounce) freezer cubes Red Bell Pepper Purée (page 42), thawed

½ avocado, pitted, peeled, and mashed

1. In a blender, combine the black beans, garlic, cumin, and red bell pepper purée. Purée until smooth. Add water as needed to thin and a pinch of herb or spice (if using).

2. Transfer the mixture to a medium pot, and heat over low heat for 10 minutes. Once the soup is warm, add the avocado.

3. Cool slightly before serving.

TIP: Adding cooked brown rice or quinoa to this recipe tastes great and provides even more heartiness and texture for your little one. Feel free to thin with low-sodium vegetable broth.

STORAGE: Store any leftovers in the refrigerator for up to 3 days.

HERBS AND SPICES: You can add paprika, fresh oregano, and mild chili powder to this recipe for added flavor.

INDIAN LENTIL STEW

• • •

YIELD: 8 (2-OUNCE) SERVINGS   **PREP TIME:** 10 MINUTES   **COOK TIME:** 5 TO 10 MINUTES

Creamy coconut milk and hearty lentils make this recipe both filling and nutritious for your baby. It's rich in protein, and with the addition of Spinach Purée (page 52), it becomes a complete meal. I often gave this to Layla for dinner to keep her full through the night.

DAIRY-FREE

GLUTEN-FREE

NUT-FREE

VEGAN

VEGETARIAN

4 (1-ounce) freezer cubes Spinach Purée (page 52), thawed

1 cup cooked lentils

½ cup coconut milk

½ teaspoon ground cumin

½ teaspoon ground coriander

1. In a medium saucepan, combine the spinach purée, lentils, coconut milk, cumin, coriander, and a pinch of herb or spice (if using). Bring to a simmer, then cook until the lentils are very soft, 5 to 10 minutes.

2. Mash half of the lentils slightly in the pot to make them easier to chew.

3. Cool slightly before serving.

TIP: Cooked quinoa or brown rice go really well with this recipe, as does plain Greek yogurt (as a topping). You can also substitute just about any vegetable purée for the spinach, or add additional veggie purées to amp up the nutritional value.

STORAGE: Store any leftovers in the refrigerator for up to 3 days.

HERBS AND SPICES: Ground turmeric and garam masala make wonderful additions.

CAULIFLOWER MASHED POTATOES

• • •

YIELD: 8 (2-OUNCE) SERVINGS   **PREP TIME:** 10 MINUTES   **COOK TIME:** 10 TO 15 MINUTES

A healthy twist on traditional mashed potatoes, this recipe replaces half the potatoes with antioxidant-rich cauliflower. It also incorporates protein and good fats in the form of full-fat plain Greek yogurt. Your baby is sure to love the tangy flavor and creamy texture of this recipe.

GLUTEN-FREE

NUT-FREE

VG

VEGETARIAN

2 potatoes, peeled and cut into ¼-inch cubes

8 (1-ounce) freezer cubes Cauliflower Purée (page 50), thawed

½ cup full-fat plain Greek yogurt

1 garlic clove, minced

1. Pour about ½ inch of water into a medium pot and set a steamer basket inside it. Add the potatoes and bring the water to a simmer over medium heat. Steam for 10 to 15 minutes, until the potatoes are soft.

2. Transfer half the potatoes to a medium bowl and mash. Add the rest of the steamed potatoes, cauliflower purée, Greek yogurt, and garlic and mix to combine.

3. Cool slightly before serving.

TIP: Add ¼ cup of shredded Cheddar cheese to this recipe for additional protein.

STORAGE: Store any leftovers in the refrigerator for up to 3 days.

CURRIED CAULIFLOWER SOUP

• • •

YIELD: 8 (2-OUNCE) SERVINGS   **PREP TIME:** 10 MINUTES   **COOK TIME:** 5 MINUTES

Give this one a try—develop baby's palate a bit with the depth of a few complementary flavors. Curry and cauliflower go exceptionally well together, and this recipe incorporates them into a milder version that's truly baby-friendly.

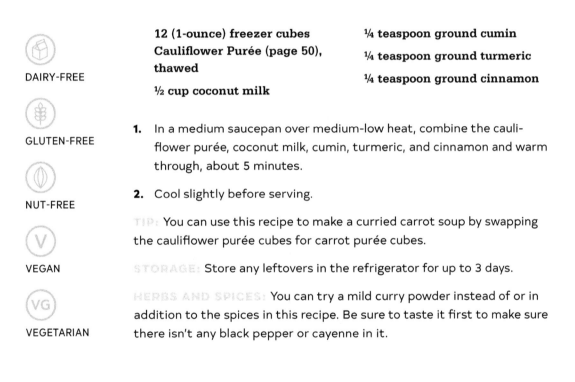

DAIRY-FREE

GLUTEN-FREE

NUT-FREE

V

VEGAN

VG

VEGETARIAN

12 (1-ounce) freezer cubes Cauliflower Purée (page 50), thawed

½ cup coconut milk

¼ teaspoon ground cumin

¼ teaspoon ground turmeric

¼ teaspoon ground cinnamon

1. In a medium saucepan over medium-low heat, combine the cauliflower purée, coconut milk, cumin, turmeric, and cinnamon and warm through, about 5 minutes.

2. Cool slightly before serving.

TIP: You can use this recipe to make a curried carrot soup by swapping the cauliflower purée cubes for carrot purée cubes.

STORAGE: Store any leftovers in the refrigerator for up to 3 days.

HERBS AND SPICES: You can try a mild curry powder instead of or in addition to the spices in this recipe. Be sure to taste it first to make sure there isn't any black pepper or cayenne in it.

LENTIL AND SWISS CHARD SOUP

• • •

YIELD: 8 (2-OUNCE) SERVINGS   **PREP TIME:** 10 MINUTES   **COOK TIME:** 5 MINUTES

This recipe calls for two purées, but as your baby gets more comfortable with chunky textures, feel free to leave the lentils whole and cooked until soft enough to chew.

DAIRY-FREE

GLUTEN-FREE

NUT-FREE

V

VEGAN

VG

VEGETARIAN

6 (1-ounce) freezer cubes Lentil Purée (page 57), thawed

6 (1-ounce) freezer cubes Swiss chard purée (see Spinach Purée, page 52), thawed

½ cup coconut milk

¼ teaspoon ground nutmeg

Pinch ground cinnamon

1. In a medium saucepan over medium-low heat, combine the lentil purée, Swiss chard purée, milk, nutmeg, and cinnamon and warm through, about 5 minutes.

2. Cool slightly before serving.

TIP: This soup tastes great mixed with whole-milk Greek yogurt, which has the added benefit of increasing the protein content of this recipe.

STORAGE: Store any leftovers in the refrigerator for up to 3 days.

PUMPKIN AND WHITE BEAN BISQUE

• • •

YIELD: 8 (2-OUNCE) SERVINGS   **PREP TIME:** 10 MINUTES   **COOK TIME:** 10 MINUTES

Pumpkin and sage are two classic fall flavors that pair beautifully. The white beans are an excellent source of protein and fiber, while the pumpkin is rich in vitamins C and E.

DAIRY-FREE

GLUTEN-FREE

NUT-FREE

VEGAN

VEGETARIAN

1 cup canned white beans, rinsed and drained

1 cup diced fresh pumpkin

1 garlic clove, minced

½ teaspoon finely chopped fresh sage

½ teaspoon ground cumin

1. In a medium saucepan over medium-low heat, combine the beans, pumpkin, garlic, sage, and cumin and warm through, about 10 minutes. Partially mash the pumpkin and white bean mixture so that it's chunky and easy to chew.

2. Cool slightly before serving.

TIP: To make this more of a soup, add a bit of low-sodium vegetable broth to the mixture before mashing.

STORAGE: Store any leftovers in the refrigerator for up to 3 days.

CHANA MASALA

• • •

YIELD: 8 (2-OUNCE) SERVINGS   **PREP TIME:** 10 MINUTES   **COOK TIME:** 5 MINUTES

Chana masala is a traditional Indian dish that's packed with nutrients, protein, fiber, and flavor. This baby-food version combines chickpeas, quinoa, and cauliflower for a chunky meal that's both filling and fun for your little one to eat.

9 TO 12 MONTHS

DAIRY-FREE

GLUTEN-FREE

NUT-FREE

(V)
VEGAN

(VG)
VEGETARIAN

1½ cups canned chickpeas, rinsed and drained

½ cup cooked quinoa

6 (1-ounce) freezer cubes Cauliflower Purée (page 50), thawed

½ cup fresh or canned crushed tomatoes

½ teaspoon ground cumin

1. In a medium saucepan over medium-low heat, combine the chickpeas, quinoa, cauliflower purée, tomatoes with their juices, and cumin and warm through, about 5 minutes. Partially mash the chickpeas to make them easier to chew.

2. Cool slightly before serving.

TIP: Try serving this dish with plain Greek yogurt—it tastes great!

STORAGE: Store any leftovers in the refrigerator for up to 3 days.

HERBS AND SPICES: For additional flavor, add ground coriander, garam masala, and turmeric. You can even try a mild curry powder in this recipe—just be sure to taste it first to make sure there isn't any black pepper or cayenne in it.

CARROT SOUP

• • •

YIELD: 8 (2-OUNCE) SERVINGS   **PREP TIME:** 10 MINUTES   **COOK TIME:** 10 MINUTES

Carrots are full of vitamin A, which is great for your baby's developing eyesight. When you pair it with rich coconut milk, warm spices, and banana, this soup is sure to be a hit with your baby's developing taste buds.

DAIRY-FREE

GLUTEN-FREE

NUT-FREE

V

VEGAN

VG

VEGETARIAN

1½ cups diced carrots

¼ teaspoon ground ginger

¼ cup coconut milk

4 (1-ounce) freezer cubes Banana Purée (page 31), thawed

1. In a medium saucepan over medium-low heat, combine the carrots, ginger, coconut milk, and banana purée and warm through until the carrots are very soft, about 10 minutes.

2. Cool slightly before serving.

TIP: Add Lentil Purée (page 57) or White Bean Purée (page 59) freezer cubes to this dish to amp up the protein.

STORAGE: Store any leftovers in the refrigerator for up to 3 days.

TOMATO, WHITE BEAN, AND VEGGIE STEW

• • •

YIELD: 12 (2-OUNCE) SERVINGS   **PREP TIME:** 10 MINUTES   **COOK TIME:** 10 MINUTES

I often made meals for Layla that were similar to ones my husband and I were already eating, so I could easily transition her to family meals when she got older. This stew is a perfect example. Initially, you can start out with the vegetable purées; as your baby gets older, you can turn this into a family meal by cooking the veggies super soft; adding spices like Italian seasoning, salt, and pepper; and topping the stew with shredded Parmesan cheese.

DAIRY-FREE

GLUTEN-FREE

NUT-FREE

Ⓥ

VEGAN

ⓋⒼ

VEGETARIAN

1 cup canned white beans, rinsed and drained

½ cup fresh or canned crushed tomatoes

4 (1-ounce) freezer cubes Zucchini Purée (page 44), thawed

4 (1-ounce) freezer cubes Red Bell Pepper Purée (page 42), thawed

4 (1-ounce) freezer cubes Spinach Purée (page 52), thawed

1. In a medium saucepan, combine the beans, tomatoes with their juices, zucchini purée, red bell pepper purée, spinach purée, and a pinch of herb or spice (if using), and warm through for about 10 minutes. Partially mash the white beans so they are easy to chew.

2. Cool slightly before serving.

TIP: You can use this stew as a topping for pasta once your baby is used to eating chunkier foods. Just cook whole-wheat pasta until it's very soft and use this recipe as the sauce. Shredded Parmesan or mozzarella cheese also works great as a topping.

STORAGE: Store any leftovers in the refrigerator for up to 3 days.

HERBS AND SPICES: I recommend adding a generous amount of Italian herbs to this dish to enhance its flavor. In particular, dried oregano, thyme, rosemary, and basil work great in this recipe.

CORN AND QUINOA CHOWDER

• • •

YIELD: 8 (2-OUNCE) SERVINGS **PREP TIME:** 10 MINUTES **COOK TIME:** 10 MINUTES

Quinoa is an extraordinary food because it contains all of the amino acids necessary to create a complete source of vegetarian protein. The veggie purées and corn in this recipe mimic the texture and flavor of a typical corn chowder. You can further enhance it by adding a splash of coconut milk to the chowder when it's done.

DAIRY-FREE

GLUTEN-FREE

NUT-FREE

VEGAN

VEGETARIAN

½ cup cooked quinoa

½ cup frozen corn kernels

4 (1-ounce) freezer cubes Sweet Potato Purée (page 48), thawed

4 (1-ounce) freezer cubes Red Bell Pepper Purée (page 42), thawed

½ teaspoon ground cumin

1. In a medium saucepan, combine the quinoa, corn, sweet potato purée, red bell pepper purée, and cumin and warm for about 10 minutes. Partially mash the corn so it is easy to chew.

2. Cool slightly before serving.

TIP: Because of their fibrous outer husks, corn kernels can sometimes be challenging for babies to chew. If that's the case with your little one, I recommend puréeing the corn before adding it to the recipe.

STORAGE: Store any leftovers in the refrigerator for up to 3 days.

WHITEFISH WITH CHOPPED GREENS SOUP

• • •

YIELD: 12 (2-OUNCE) SERVINGS   **PREP TIME:** 10 MINUTES   **COOK TIME:** 20 MINUTES

This slightly sweet soup is made of puréed greens and apples with little bits of flaked whitefish mixed in, resulting in a tasty mix that's also an excellent source of protein and fiber. The recipe calls for kale, but feel free to substitute any greens you have on hand.

FREEZER-FRIENDLY

DAIRY-FREE

GLUTEN-FREE

NUT-FREE

2 teaspoons olive oil, plus more if needed

3 ounces whitefish, such as cod, skin and bones removed, cut into ¼-inch pieces

1 cup chopped kale (leafy parts only)

1 apple, peeled, cored, and cut into ¼-inch pieces

1 cup water or low-sodium vegetable broth

Pinch ground sage

1. In a small pot over medium-high heat, heat the olive oil until it shimmers. Add the fish and cook until it is white, 5 to 7 minutes. Remove and set aside.

2. In the same pot, cook the kale, stirring until it is soft, about 7 minutes. (If the pot is dry before you add the kale, add another teaspoon of olive oil.)

3. Add the apple, water, and sage. Bring to a simmer. Cook, stirring occasionally, until the apple is soft, adding more water if needed.

4. Transfer to a blender or food processor and purée, being careful to avoid splashing any hot liquid. Pour the purée back into the pot, add the fish, and reheat for 1 to 2 minutes. Cool slightly before serving.

TIP: Thin as needed with additional water or broth before adding the fish.

STORAGE: Refrigerate, tightly sealed, for up to 3 days, or freeze for up to 3 months.

GROUND TURKEY AND BLACK BEAN STEW

• • •

YIELD: 8 (2-OUNCE) SERVINGS   PREP TIME: 10 MINUTES   COOK TIME: 20 MINUTES

This simple stew gives little teeth and gums something soft to chew on, and it contains tasty veggies and a simple sauce that is both flavorful and nutritious.

FREEZER-FRIENDLY

DAIRY-FREE

GLUTEN-FREE

NUT-FREE

2 teaspoons olive oil

1 carrot, peeled and cut into ¼-inch-cubes

4 ounces ground turkey

4 ounces (about ⅓ cup) canned black beans, rinsed and drained

¼ teaspoon dried thyme

¼ teaspoon garlic powder

1 cup low-sodium chicken broth

1 teaspoon cornstarch or arrowroot powder

1. In a small nonstick skillet over medium-high heat, heat the olive oil until it shimmers.

2. Add the carrot and cook, stirring occasionally, until it is soft, about 5 minutes. Remove the carrot and set aside.

3. Add the ground turkey to the skillet and cook, stirring occasionally and crumbling into small bits, until it is well cooked, about 5 minutes.

4. Add the black beans, cooked carrot, thyme, and garlic powder. Cook, stirring, until the beans are heated through, 3 to 4 minutes.

5. In a small bowl, whisk together the chicken broth and cornstarch. Add to the skillet and cook, stirring, until it thickens, 1 to 2 minutes more.

TIP: You can use any ground meat here. As you cook, use a spoon to continuously crumble the meat until the pieces are very small. You can also replace the fresh carrot with thawed frozen chopped carrot and add it when you add the black beans.

STORAGE: Refrigerate, tightly sealed, for up to 3 days, or freeze for up to 3 months.

9 TO 12 MONTHS

PEA SOUP WITH HAM

• • •

YIELD: 12 (2-OUNCE) SERVINGS   **PREP TIME:** 5 MINUTES   **COOK TIME:** 10 MINUTES

Frozen peas make this thick and tasty soup a snap. You can adjust the consistency with any liquid you choose, including breast milk, formula, water, broth, or even yogurt.

FREEZER-FRIENDLY

DAIRY-FREE

GLUTEN-FREE

NUT-FREE

2 cups frozen peas

1 cup water or low-sodium chicken broth

¼ teaspoon onion powder

¼ teaspoon dried tarragon

3 ounces ham, finely diced

1. Put the peas, water, onion powder, and tarragon in a small pot. Bring to a simmer over medium-high heat, and cook until the peas are soft, about 5 minutes.

2. Transfer the mixture to a blender or food processor and purée. Add more water if desired to reach your needed consistency.

3. Return the purée to the pot and stir in the ham. Bring to a simmer, stirring, and heat through for about 3 minutes.

4. Cool slightly before serving.

TIP: You can reserve about ¼ cup of the cooked peas (before puréeing) and add them when you add the ham, giving your baby some extra bits to chew on.

STORAGE: Refrigerate, tightly sealed, for up to 3 days, or freeze for up to 3 months.

GROUND BEEF AND SWEET POTATO SOUP

• • •

YIELD: 12 (2-OUNCE SERVINGS)   **PREP TIME:** 10 MINUTES   **COOK TIME:** 25 MINUTES

This cozy soup has a base of sweet potato purée that you'll thin with water or broth. You can give the soup an additional boost of flavor by using the same pot to cook both the ground beef and the sweet potato.

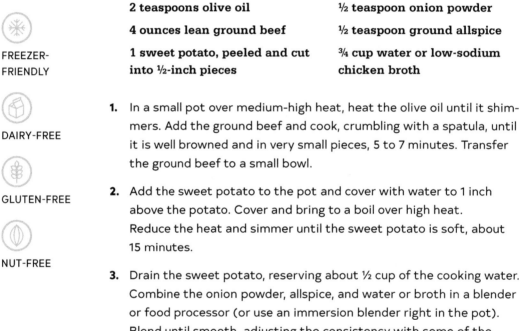

FREEZER-FRIENDLY

DAIRY-FREE

GLUTEN-FREE

NUT-FREE

2 teaspoons olive oil

4 ounces lean ground beef

1 sweet potato, peeled and cut into ½-inch pieces

½ teaspoon onion powder

½ teaspoon ground allspice

¾ cup water or low-sodium chicken broth

1. In a small pot over medium-high heat, heat the olive oil until it shimmers. Add the ground beef and cook, crumbling with a spatula, until it is well browned and in very small pieces, 5 to 7 minutes. Transfer the ground beef to a small bowl.

2. Add the sweet potato to the pot and cover with water to 1 inch above the potato. Cover and bring to a boil over high heat. Reduce the heat and simmer until the sweet potato is soft, about 15 minutes.

3. Drain the sweet potato, reserving about ½ cup of the cooking water. Combine the onion powder, allspice, and water or broth in a blender or food processor (or use an immersion blender right in the pot). Blend until smooth, adjusting the consistency with some of the reserved cooking water, if desired. Return the purée to the pot over medium heat.

4. Add the cooked ground beef. Simmer for 3 minutes, stirring constantly.

5. Cool slightly before serving.

FINGER FOOD READY

● ● ●

Most babies are ready for finger foods at around eight months of age. Some cues you can look for that indicate your child's readiness to feed himself include a firmer pincer grasp (thumb and forefinger), which enables him to pick up small objects; his ability to "chew" using his gums to mash food; and his ability to sit up unassisted in a high chair. Once your baby has reached these milestones, you can offer tiny finger foods at each meal to give your baby practice. You'll still be feeding him most of his food, but it's important to give him the opportunity to feed himself as well.

It's best to start with simple, single-ingredient finger foods. Easy options include diced raw fruits, like banana, avocado, mango, and melon, as well as soft-baked or steamed fruits or vegetables. Tofu cubes, soft-cooked pasta (not al dente), small chunks of soft cheeses, scrambled egg yolks, and baby bite-size pieces of toast are all great choices. In the early days, you'll want to avoid foods that might be choking hazards. That means holding off on dried fruits (including raisins); whole nuts and seeds; fruits and veggies that are firm when raw, such as carrots and apples; small, round foods such as grapes or cheese-stick rounds; and foods that are hard to chew, such as popcorn.

TIP: If puréeing the hot ingredients in a blender or food processor, be careful. Allow steam to escape through the top opening while you blend, and hold the lid in place with a folded towel to protect your hand. If you don't allow steam to escape, hot liquids can explode out of the blender or food processor.

STORAGE: Refrigerate, tightly sealed, for up to 3 days, or freeze for up to 3 months.

NUT BUTTER AND BANANA STACKERS

• • •

YIELD: 1 SERVING **PREP TIME:** 10 MINUTES

A meal doesn't always have to be meat and potatoes. Nut butter "stackers" can be ready in no time, and there are near-infinite twists on this concept. This is a lifesaver when you want a fun, interesting, and nutritious meal but don't have time to cook. Note: Nut butter foods should wait until baby turns one, when she's adept enough to swallow this sticky ingredient.

9 TO 12 MONTHS

DAIRY-FREE

VEGAN

VG

VEGETARIAN

1 slice sprouted-wheat bread, crusts cut off

1 tablespoon nut butter (peanut, almond, etc.)

⅓ banana, sliced

1. Toast the bread slightly so it's still soft. Spread the nut butter on the bread.

2. Cut the bread into 1-inch squares.

3. Top each square with a banana slice and serve.

TIP: Experiment with different soft fruits on the nut butter cubes. Partially cooked apples, pears, or berries work well for these fun snacks. You can also use the basic stacker concept to experiment with different flavor combinations (e.g., hummus with soft carrots, cream cheese with avocado, and so on).

PASTA WITH VEGGIES AND WHITE BEANS

● ● ●

YIELD: 8 (3-OUNCE) SERVINGS   **PREP TIME:** 10 MINUTES   **COOK TIME:** 15 MINUTES

Whole-wheat pasta is a great finger food because it's a breeze to make and easy for your baby to pick up. I like cutting up pasta into bite-size pieces and combining it with mixed veggies and white beans for a complete meal. On a practical note, if you don't want your child to get too messy, you may choose to skip the crushed tomatoes in this recipe—otherwise, pull out your camera.

DAIRY-FREE

NUT-FREE

(V)

VEGAN

(VG)

VEGETARIAN

½ cup dried whole-wheat or other whole-grain pasta (like penne)

1 cup (from 1 [16-ounce] package) frozen mixed vegetables (like carrots, peas, green beans, and corn)

1 teaspoon dried Italian seasoning

½ cup fresh or canned crushed tomatoes

½ cup canned white beans, rinsed and drained

Grated Parmesan cheese (optional)

1. In a small pot of boiling water, cook the pasta until it is very soft. Drain, cool slightly, then cut into small pieces.

2. While the pasta is cooking, pour about ½ inch of water into another small pot fitted with a steamer basket, and add the mixed vegetables. Bring to a simmer over medium heat and steam until soft, 10 to 15 minutes.

3. In a medium skillet over medium-low heat, combine the cooked pasta, vegetables, Italian seasoning, tomatoes with their juices, and white beans, and heat until warmed through. Sprinkle with Parmesan cheese (if using), and serve warm.

STORAGE: Refrigerate for up to 3 days.

YAM AND SQUASH "FRIES"

• • •

YIELD: 4 SERVINGS **PREP TIME:** 10 MINUTES **COOK TIME:** 15 TO 20 MINUTES

Soft-cooked vegetables were one of my go-to finger foods. After experimenting with different shapes and sizes, I found these "fries" were really easy for Layla to pick up and eat on her own. Try serving these with hummus or herb-seasoned yogurt to make them even more enticing to young eaters. Although both yams and sweet potatoes work for this recipe, I prefer yams because of their deeper flavor and beta-carotene boost.

DAIRY-FREE

GLUTEN-FREE

NUT-FREE

VEGAN

VEGETARIAN

Olive oil spray

1 small yam, peeled and cut into ¼-inch matchsticks

1 zucchini or yellow squash, seeded and cut into ¼-inch matchsticks

1 tablespoon olive oil

¼ teaspoon garlic powder

¼ teaspoon paprika

Several pinches kosher salt

1. Preheat the oven to 450°F. Coat a medium baking sheet with olive oil spray, or line it with parchment paper.

2. In a small bowl, combine the yam, zucchini, olive oil, garlic powder, paprika, and salt and toss to coat.

3. Spread the vegetable mixture on the prepared baking sheet in a single layer. Bake until the yam is lightly browned and fork-tender, 15 to 20 minutes.

TIP: Substitute butternut squash for the sweet potato. You can also try fresh herbs like oregano and thyme, or ground allspice and cinnamon with these fries instead of the garlic powder and paprika.

STORAGE: Store extra fries in the refrigerator for up to 3 days.

ROASTED VEGGIE CUBES

• • •

YIELD: 4 SERVINGS   **PREP TIME:** 10 MINUTES   **COOK TIME:** 15 TO 20 MINUTES

Cumin and coriander add a hint of warmth to these roasted vegetables, but go ahead and add any spice combination you like. Feel free to substitute other squashes or vegetables in this recipe; roasted green beans and asparagus are delicious, too.

9 TO 12 MONTHS

DAIRY-FREE

GLUTEN-FREE

NUT-FREE

(V) VEGAN

(VG) VEGETARIAN

Olive oil spray

1 carrot, peeled and cut into ¼-inch cubes

½ medium butternut squash, peeled, seeded, and cut into ¼-inch cubes

1 beet, peeled and cut into ¼-inch cubes

1 tablespoon olive oil

½ teaspoon ground cumin

½ teaspoon ground coriander

Pinch kosher salt

1. Preheat the oven to 450°F. Coat a medium baking sheet with olive oil spray, or line it with parchment paper.

2. In a small bowl, combine the carrot, butternut squash, beet, olive oil, cumin, coriander, and salt. Toss to coat.

3. Spread the mixture on the prepared baking sheet in a single layer. Bake until the vegetables are lightly browned and fork-tender, 15 to 20 minutes.

TIP: Carrots, winter squashes, and beets are all rather hard and dense when raw. To cut them into small dice, first peel them, then cut long, flat slices that are about ¼-inch thick. Lay the slices flat on your cutting board, then cut those lengthwise into ¼-inch strips. Cut those strips crosswise so that you end up with little cubes. They don't have to be perfect. The idea is to make them as uniform as reasonably possible so that they cook at about the same rate.

STORAGE: Store the veggie cubes in the refrigerator for up to 3 days.

HERBS AND SPICES: Mix up your flavors by replacing the warm spices with Italian herbs like oregano, thyme, or rosemary.

TOFU NUGGETS

• • •

YIELD: 4 SERVINGS   **PREP TIME:** 10 MINUTES   **COOK TIME:** 30 MINUTES

Tofu is an excellent source of plant-based protein, and these nuggets are a fun, mess-free treat. The whole-wheat flour (or cornmeal or oat flour) adds a good dose of fiber and healthy complex carbohydrates. Look to the tip for dipping ideas.

DAIRY-FREE

NUT-FREE

(V)

VEGAN

(VG)

VEGETARIAN

1 (16-ounce) package extra-firm tofu

¼ cup olive oil

1 cup whole-wheat flour, fine cornmeal, or oat flour

½ teaspoon garlic powder

½ teaspoon onion powder

Pinch kosher salt

1. Preheat the oven to 400°F. Line a medium baking sheet with parchment paper.

2. Drain the tofu and press it with paper towels to get rid of as much excess water as possible. Cut it into 1-inch cubes.

3. Pour the olive oil into a small bowl. In a zip-top bag, combine the flour, garlic powder, onion powder, and salt. Take several tofu cubes, dunk them in the olive oil, then put them in the bag and shake to coat the tofu with the flour and spice mixture. Repeat with the remaining tofu.

4. Place the tofu nuggets on the prepared baking sheet. Bake for 15 minutes, flip the tofu nuggets, and bake for about 15 minutes more or until lightly browned and crispy on top.

TIP: These nuggets can be served with ketchup, barbecue sauce, or low-sodium soy sauce for dipping. And if you'd like to make your own oat flour, it's easy to do. Just put rolled oats into the food processor and pulse until a fine flour forms; use gluten-free rolled oats to make the flour gluten-free.

STORAGE: Store in the refrigerator for up to 3 days.

SCRAMBLED EGG YOLKS WITH VEGGIES

• • •

YIELD: 4 SERVINGS   **PREP TIME:** 10 MINUTES   **COOK TIME:** 10 MINUTES

Egg yolks are rarely allergenic, which is why this recipe calls for just the yolks instead of whole eggs. Once your baby turns a year old, feel free to introduce egg whites and prepare this yummy scramble with whole eggs.

GLUTEN-FREE

NUT-FREE

VG

VEGETARIAN

4 eggs

1 teaspoon olive oil

1 cup chopped cooked vegetables, like broccoli, bell peppers, spinach, or carrots

¼ teaspoon garlic powder

½ teaspoon dried oregano

1. Crack the eggs and separate the whites from the yolks. Reserve the whites for another use.

2. In a medium skillet over medium heat, warm the olive oil.

3. In a small bowl, beat the yolks. Add the vegetables, garlic powder, and oregano and stir to combine.

4. Pour the egg and vegetable mixture into the skillet.

5. Cook over medium heat, stirring constantly, until the yolks are scrambled and set. Let cool just slightly and serve.

TIP: To serve leftovers, reheat gently in the microwave until just warm.

BROCCOLI AND CHEESE NUGGETS

• • •

YIELD: 8 SERVINGS   **PREP TIME:** 10 MINUTES   **COOK TIME:** 20 MINUTES

Crispy on the outside and soft on the inside, these nuggets are perfect for little hands. They're packed with antioxidants from the broccoli, protein from the cheese and eggs, and fiber from the wheat germ (or oat flour), making this a complete mini-meal that will keep your baby full and satisfied.

NUT-FREE

VG

VEGETARIAN

2 eggs

1 (16-ounce) package frozen broccoli, steamed and chopped into very small pieces

½ cup wheat germ or oat flour

½ cup shredded Cheddar cheese

2 garlic cloves, minced

1. Preheat the oven to 400°F. Line a medium baking sheet with parchment paper.

2. In a small bowl, beat the eggs. Add the broccoli, wheat germ, cheese, and garlic. Mix well to combine.

3. Form the broccoli mixture into ½-inch balls. Place the balls on the prepared baking sheet.

4. Bake for about 20 minutes or until lightly browned and crispy on top.

TIP: You can make the oat flour yourself by taking rolled oats and pulsing them in a food processor; use gluten-free rolled oats to make the flour gluten-free. You can also replace the Cheddar cheese with Parmesan for a slightly different flavor.

STORAGE: Store in the refrigerator for up to 3 days.

MINI BANANA-BLUEBERRY PANCAKES

• • •

YIELD: ABOUT 8 (3-INCH) PANCAKES   **PREP TIME:** 10 MINUTES   **COOK TIME:** 10 MINUTES

You won't believe how delicious these flourless pancakes are. To amp up the fiber and healthy fats, add 1 tablespoon ground flaxseed to the batter. If you want to keep things super simple, you can leave out the berries and spices and make banana pancakes with just the banana and eggs.

GLUTEN-FREE

NUT-FREE

VG

VEGETARIAN

½ cup fresh or frozen blueberries

1 banana

2 eggs, beaten

¼ teaspoon ground cinnamon

¼ teaspoon ground nutmeg

Olive oil spray

1. If you're using frozen blueberries, thaw them a little ahead of time, allowing the water or juices to drain off.

2. In a small bowl, mash the banana. Add the eggs, blueberries, cinnamon, and nutmeg and mix well.

3. Heat a griddle over medium heat and coat it with olive oil spray.

4. Pour about 2 tablespoons of batter for each pancake onto the griddle. Cook until bubbles form on top of the pancakes, 2 to 3 minutes. Flip and cook on the other side for another 2 to 3 minutes. Serve warm.

TIP: I like serving these pancakes with almond butter spread on top, but any nut butter will work well. You can also top them with any fruit purée as a healthier alternative to jam or maple syrup—pear purée in particular tastes great.

HEALTHY OAT BREAKFAST COOKIES

• • •

YIELD: ABOUT 16 COOKIES   **PREP TIME:** 10 MINUTES   **COOK TIME:** 15 MINUTES

These cookies contain nut butter, so they are best reserved for the "over-one" crowd, but they're perfect for little hands, and you can cut them up into smaller, bite-size pieces as well. They freeze well and are a healthy grab-and-go breakfast option for anyone in the family, so make some extra!

DAIRY-FREE

VEGAN

VEGETARIAN

Olive oil spray or 1 teaspoon olive oil

2 medium ripe bananas, mashed

2 tablespoons peanut butter (or any nut butter)

1 cup uncooked quick oats or rolled oats

¼ cup crushed walnuts

¼ teaspoon ground cinnamon

1. Preheat the oven to 350°F. Coat a medium nonstick baking sheet with olive oil spray or olive oil.

2. In a medium bowl, combine the mashed bananas and peanut butter. Add the oats and mix until thoroughly combined. Add the walnuts and cinnamon. Scoop 1 rounded tablespoon of batter onto the prepared baking sheet. Repeat with the remaining batter.

3. Bake for 15 minutes or until golden.

TIP: You can use this recipe to make healthy granola bars for your little one. Instead of shaping the dough into cookies, shape them into small rectangles for a granola bar snack!

SAVORY SWEET POTATO, LENTIL, AND CARROT CAKES

• • •

YIELD: 8 CAKES   **PREP TIME:** 10 MINUTES   **COOK TIME:** 10 MINUTES

These cakes get their inspiration from latkes—shredded-potato cakes that are traditionally fried—but this version is much healthier and more nutritious for your baby. Packed with protein from the lentils and vitamin A from the sweet potatoes and carrots, this recipe is a nutritional powerhouse for growing bodies.

9 TO 12 MONTHS

DAIRY-FREE

NUT-FREE

VG

VEGETARIAN

1 cup peeled and shredded sweet potato

1 cup peeled and shredded carrot

½ cup cooked lentils, mashed

4 eggs

4 teaspoons whole-wheat flour, oat flour, or coconut flour

Pinch kosher salt

Olive oil spray

1. In a large bowl, combine the sweet potato, carrot, and lentils.

2. In a small bowl, whisk the eggs.

3. Add the flour to the sweet potato mixture, stirring to combine. Add the eggs and salt to the mixture and stir well.

4. Heat a large skillet over medium heat, and coat it with olive oil spray. Divide the sweet potato mixture into 8 parts, spooning each part onto the skillet. Flatten the cakes lightly with a spatula. Cook until the bottom is golden brown, about 5 minutes. Flip each cake and cook the other side until it is browned and crispy, another 5 minutes.

5. Cool before serving, cutting each cake into smaller pieces for bite-size chunks.

TIP: To make these cakes even more flavorful, try adding ground cumin, cinnamon, allspice, ground ginger, or nutmeg to the mixture before cooking.

PUMPKIN MAC AND CHEESE

• • •

YIELD: 8 (½-CUP) SERVINGS   **PREP TIME:** 10 MINUTES   **COOK TIME:** 10 TO 15 MINUTES

This healthy twist on traditional cheese sauce tastes great over whole-wheat macaroni; the pumpkin adds a rich, sweet flavor that pairs beautifully with the Cheddar cheese. Broccoli adds a hefty dose of antioxidants and fiber to this cozy and nourishing dish.

NUT-FREE

VG

VEGETARIAN

1 medium pumpkin, peeled, seeded, and cut into 1-inch cubes

½ cup dried whole-wheat macaroni

¼ cup whole milk, plus more if needed

½ cup shredded Cheddar cheese

½ cup broccoli florets, steamed and cut into small pieces

Salt

Freshly ground black pepper

1. Pour about ½ inch of water into a medium pot and set a steamer basket inside it. Arrange the pumpkin evenly inside the basket. Bring the water to a simmer over medium heat and steam for 10 to 15 minutes, until the pumpkin is soft.

2. Meanwhile, cook the macaroni according to the package directions. Drain immediately.

3. Transfer the steamed pumpkin to a blender, add the milk and cheese, and purée until smooth. Add more milk to thin the sauce, if desired.

4. In a large bowl, combine the macaroni and broccoli with the pumpkin sauce, add salt and pepper to taste, and serve warm.

TIP: You can use butternut squash or even cauliflower in place of the pumpkin in this recipe.

ORZO WITH GROUND TURKEY AND ZUCCHINI

• • •

YIELD: 6 (½-CUP) SERVINGS **PREP TIME:** 10 MINUTES **COOK TIME:** 15 MINUTES

Cooked orzo is the perfect starter pasta for little ones who are just getting used to chewing solid food. While you may wind up with some pasta on the floor, this is a fairly "dry" recipe (no sauce), which means relatively easy cleanup of your baby and her surroundings.

FREEZER-FRIENDLY

DAIRY-FREE

NUT-FREE

1 tablespoon olive oil

4 ounces ground turkey

¼ cup finely chopped onion

1 small zucchini, peeled and cut into ¼-inch cubes

1 garlic clove, minced

1 cup cooked orzo

1. In a small nonstick skillet over medium-high heat, heat the olive oil until it shimmers.

2. Add the ground turkey and cook, crumbling, until it is browned, about 5 minutes. Using a slotted spoon, remove the turkey and set aside on a plate.

3. Add the onion and zucchini to the skillet and cook, stirring occasionally, until the vegetables are soft, about 5 minutes.

4. Return the turkey to the skillet and add the garlic. Cook, stirring constantly, until the garlic is fragrant, about 30 seconds.

5. Toss in the orzo and cook to heat through, about 2 minutes.

TIP: To make this dish gluten-free, replace the orzo with cooked brown rice.

STORAGE: Refrigerate, tightly sealed, for up to 3 days, or freeze for up to 3 months.

SALMON AND SWEET POTATO CAKES

• • •

YIELD: 12 CAKES   **PREP TIME:** 15 MINUTES   **COOK TIME:** 30 MINUTES

While the recipe calls for salmon, any pink-fleshed fish, such as trout or steelhead, will work. Be sure to sift through the fish carefully and remove all the pinbones, and flake the cooked fish into very small pieces so it is easy for your baby to chew.

FREEZER-FRIENDLY

DAIRY-FREE

GLUTEN-FREE

NUT-FREE

4 ounces salmon

½ sweet potato, peeled and cut into 1-inch cubes

½ teaspoon chopped fresh dill

¼ teaspoon onion powder

1 egg, lightly beaten

2 tablespoons olive oil

1. In a small saucepan, bring about 1 cup of water to a simmer, and poach the salmon for 7 to 10 minutes. Remove the salmon from the water and allow it to cool a bit. Remove the skin and any pinbones, then flake the fish with a fork.

2. In a small pot, cover the sweet potato with water and bring to a boil. Boil until the potato is soft, about 10 minutes.

3. Transfer the potato to a medium bowl and mash. Add the dill and onion powder.

4. Stir in the egg and the poached salmon. Mix until well combined.

5. In a large nonstick skillet over medium-high heat, heat the olive oil until it shimmers.

6. Form the potato-salmon mixture into 12 balls, then flatten them and place in the skillet. Cook in the hot oil until browned on both sides, about 5 minutes per side.

TIP: You can also replace the fresh salmon with canned wild salmon or ground meat such as turkey or chicken.

STORAGE: Refrigerate, tightly sealed, for up to 3 days, or freeze for up to 3 months.

CHICKEN AND WHITE BEAN FRITTERS

• • •

YIELD: 12 FRITTERS   **PREP TIME:** 15 MINUTES   **COOK TIME:** 15 MINUTES

White beans make up the binding agent in these delectable chicken fritters. An excellent source of protein and carbohydrates, these tasty treats are great for tiny fingers—and bigger fingers, too.

FREEZER-FRIENDLY

DAIRY-FREE

GLUTEN-FREE

NUT-FREE

1 teaspoon olive oil, plus 2 tablespoons used later

1 medium carrot, peeled and grated

1 cup canned white beans, rinsed and drained

¼ teaspoon dried thyme

¼ teaspoon garlic powder

4 ounces ground chicken, browned and drained

1. In a small sauté pan or skillet over medium-high heat, heat 1 teaspoon of olive oil until it shimmers. Add the carrot and cook, stirring occasionally, until soft, about 5 minutes. Allow to cool completely.

2. Transfer the carrot to a blender or food processor. Add the beans, thyme, and garlic powder and purée.

3. Transfer the purée to a medium bowl and stir in the cooked chicken. Form the mixture into 12 small balls. Press the balls flat into patties.

4. In a large nonstick skillet over medium-high heat, heat the remaining 2 tablespoons of olive oil until it shimmers.

5. Place the patties in the skillet and cook until browned on both sides, about 4 minutes per side.

6. Cool slightly before serving.

TIP: Make these patties vegetarian by eliminating the ground chicken and instead stirring in about ½ cup cooked brown rice.

STORAGE: Refrigerate, tightly sealed, for up to 3 days, or freeze for up to 3 months.

ROTINI WITH BEEF AND PUMPKIN BOLOGNESE

● ● ●

YIELD: 6 (½-CUP) SERVINGS   **PREP TIME:** 10 MINUTES   **COOK TIME:** 15 MINUTES

A typical Bolognese contains beef slow-cooked in dairy until it is fall-apart tender and deeply flavorful. This tasty, quick version is sure to delight your baby and will delight you, too, with all its vitamin A and protein.

❄
FREEZER-FRIENDLY

🥛
DAIRY-FREE

◊
NUT-FREE

1 teaspoon olive oil

4 ounces ground beef

¼ cup finely chopped onion

1 garlic clove, minced

1 cup Pumpkin Purée (page 49) or canned pumpkin purée

¼ cup water or low-sodium broth

¼ teaspoon ground sage

¾ cup rotini, cooked according to package directions and drained

1. In a small pot over medium-high heat, heat the olive oil until it shimmers. Add the ground beef and cook, stirring and crumbling, until browned, 5 to 7 minutes.

2. Add the onion and cook, stirring occasionally, until the onion is soft, 3 to 5 minutes more.

3. Add the garlic and cook, stirring constantly, for 30 seconds.

4. Add the pumpkin purée, then add the water 1 tablespoon at a time until you achieve your desired consistency. Stir in the sage and simmer for about 2 minutes more.

5. Add the rotini and heat through.

TIP: You can replace the pumpkin purée with either Butternut Squash Purée (page 47) or Carrot Purée (page 41).

STORAGE: Refrigerate, tightly sealed, for up to 3 days, or freeze for up to 3 months. If using previously frozen purée, refreeze only if it was thawed properly in the refrigerator and within 24 hours of thawing, for food safety reasons.

Avocado Toast, page 152

Chapter Six

BIG-KID MEALS

12 TO 36 MONTHS

Congratulations! Your baby has turned one and is now officially a toddler. This was one of my favorite stages with Layla. Toddlers at this age are interactive, curious, and funny, but haven't quite hit the more challenging "terrible twos" or "threenager" years yet. At this point your little one has probably been eating solids for about six months, so she's probably very used to purées and even comfortable with chunky finger foods. She might even have a few teeth by now. Continue to offer your little one a variety of foods (including purées from time to time), even if she is becoming pickier about what she will eat. It's important that babies continue to expand their palates as they get older. If your child is still breastfeeding, offer breast milk as a supplement to solid meals (in between meals) instead of as a meal itself. If your child has moved on to whole milk, offer water with her meals and milk in between meals. Now is the time to start moving away from the bottle, so you can start offering both water and milk in a sippy cup.

Although these recipes were created with toddlers in mind, many of them can be enjoyed by the whole family. I've included tips and suggestions so you can vary the flavors to accommodate your family's preferences.

HOW OFTEN: 3 solid meals
and 1 or 2 snacks per day

WHAT TO EAT: Toddler meals

HOW MUCH: 3 to 6 ounces
per meal

FINGER FOODS: Well-cooked
beans, steamed veggies, pasta
or noodles, soft raw fruit,
scrambled eggs

WHAT TO DRINK: Water
or whole milk

EASY SAUSAGE SCRAMBLE

· · ·

YIELD: 4 SERVINGS **PREP TIME:** 5 MINUTES **COOK TIME:** 10 MINUTES

Scrambled eggs are a great breakfast for big kids of all ages because they are so easy to eat and are packed with protein. Making your own sausage is quick and easy, and this meal as a whole is tasty enough to appeal to other family members as well.

FREEZER-
FRIENDLY

DAIRY-FREE

GLUTEN-FREE

NUT-FREE

2 ounces ground pork

2 ounces ground turkey

½ teaspoon dried sage

½ teaspoon garlic powder

¼ teaspoon sea salt

4 eggs, beaten

1. In a small bowl, combine the ground pork, ground turkey, sage, garlic powder, and salt. Mix well.

2. Heat a medium nonstick skillet over medium-high heat. Add the ground meat mixture and cook, crumbling with a spoon, until it is browned, about 5 minutes.

3. Add the eggs. Cook, stirring and scrambling, until the eggs are set, about 5 minutes more.

TIP: If you'd prefer, you can use all ground turkey or all ground pork, but keep in mind that ground pork is much fattier than ground turkey. If you use only ground turkey, add 2 teaspoons olive oil to the skillet before you cook it.

STORAGE: Refrigerate, tightly sealed, for up to 3 days, or freeze for up to 3 months.

GRITS WITH BABY SHRIMP

• • •

YIELD: 4 SERVINGS   **PREP TIME:** 5 MINUTES   **COOK TIME:** 10 MINUTES

It's never too soon to get your little one started on the delightful combination of shrimp and grits. Baby shrimp make this friendly for small mouths, while quick-cooking grits make it a snap to prepare. Perhaps double this recipe, as baby won't be the only one interested.

GLUTEN-FREE

NUT-FREE

4 ounces fresh or canned baby shrimp

1 tablespoon olive oil

1 garlic clove, minced

2 cups water

½ cup quick-cooking grits

¼ cup grated Cheddar cheese

2 teaspoons unsalted butter

1. Check the shrimp to make sure they smell fresh; if you detect any stale odors, put them in a fine strainer and rinse under cold water for a few seconds. Shake off the excess water and proceed with the recipe.

2. In a small nonstick skillet over medium-high heat, heat the olive oil until it shimmers.

3. Add the shrimp and cook until heated through, about 2 minutes.

4. Add the garlic and cook, stirring constantly, for 30 seconds. Set the cooked shrimp aside.

5. In a small saucepan, bring the water to a boil. Slowly stir in the grits.

6. Cook, stirring constantly, until the grits thicken, 5 to 7 minutes (or according to package directions). Stir in the cheese and butter.

7. Serve the shrimp spooned over the grits.

TIP: Any cheese will do here. To make it dairy-free, leave out the cheese and butter altogether.

STORAGE: Refrigerate for up to 3 days. This dish won't freeze well, but it is tasty enough for the whole family, so you can double the recipe if you wish.

12 TO 36 MONTHS

HAM, EGG, AND SPINACH SCRAMBLE

• • •

YIELD: 4 SERVINGS **PREP TIME:** 10 MINUTES **COOK TIME:** 10 MINUTES

With a little extra seasoning for adult portions, this dish is sure to be a hit with the whole family. It's a good source of iron, protein, and vitamins and a hearty way to start the day. Feel free to substitute any greens for the baby spinach.

DAIRY-FREE

GLUTEN-FREE

NUT-FREE

1 tablespoon olive oil

1 cup chopped baby spinach

4 ounces ham, finely chopped

1 garlic clove, minced

4 eggs, beaten

Pinch salt

1. In a small nonstick skillet, heat the olive oil over medium-high heat until it shimmers.

2. Add the spinach and ham, and cook until the spinach is soft, 3 to 4 minutes.

3. Add the garlic and cook for 30 seconds, stirring constantly.

4. Add the eggs and salt and cook, stirring, until the eggs are set, 3 to 4 minutes more.

TIP: You can add 1 to 2 tablespoons grated cheese to the eggs as they finish cooking.

STORAGE: Refrigerate for up to 3 days. This dish won't freeze well, but it is tasty enough for the whole family, so you can double the recipe if you wish.

TOFU SCRAMBLE

● ● ●

YIELD: 4 SERVINGS   **PREP TIME:** 10 MINUTES   **COOK TIME:** 15 MINUTES

This protein-packed dish is an ideal egg-free, vegan option for a breakfast scramble. Tofu takes on the flavor of whatever veggies and spices you add to it, so experiment and have some fun with this. I often make this as a "breakfast-for-dinner" dish when I'm pressed for time.

DAIRY-FREE

GLUTEN-FREE

NUT-FREE

(V)

VEGAN

(VG)

VEGETARIAN

1 tablespoon olive oil

1 red bell pepper, seeded and cut into ¼-inch dice

1 carrot, peeled and cut into ¼-inch dice

1 zucchini, cut into ¼-inch dice

¼ red onion, finely chopped

8 ounces firm tofu, cut into 1-inch cubes

Kosher salt

1. In a large saucepan over medium heat, heat the olive oil. Add the bell pepper, carrot, zucchini, and onion and cook, stirring until the vegetables begin to caramelize, 5 to 10 minutes.

2. Add the tofu, salt to taste, and a pinch of herb or spice (if using). Break up the tofu with a spatula until it has a scrambled-egg consistency. Cook for about 5 minutes or until lightly browned.

3. Cool slightly before serving.

TIP: Try replacing the tofu with tempeh for another meat-free alternative.

STORAGE: Store any leftovers in the refrigerator for up to 3 days.

HERBS AND SPICES: This scramble tastes great with fresh herbs like oregano, dill, and basil, but you can also make a more Southwestern-inspired scramble by adding cumin, paprika, and mild chili powder. A minced garlic clove will enhance either of these preparations.

PEANUT BUTTER AND BANANA OATMEAL

• • •

YIELD: 4 SERVINGS   **PREP TIME:** 5 MINUTES   **COOK TIME:** 25 MINUTES

Oatmeal is one of my favorite breakfasts. In addition to being health-supportive and filling for little tummies, it's a perfect base for a variety of toppings. This particular oatmeal reminds me of the peanut butter banana sandwiches I used to eat as a child. To save time, cook a batch of rolled oats in advance (it will keep for about 4 days in the refrigerator), so all you have to do in the morning is heat it up and mix in the bananas and peanut butter.

GLUTEN-FREE

VEGETARIAN

1 cup water

1 cup whole milk

½ cup rolled oats

1 banana, sliced

2 tablespoons peanut butter (or any nut butter of your choosing)

1. In a small pot, bring the water and milk to a boil.

2. Stir in the oats and a pinch of spice (if using), then reduce the heat to low. Cover and simmer until the oats are soft, about 20 minutes.

3. During the last 5 minutes of cooking, stir in the banana.

4. Once the banana and oats have cooked together, stir in the peanut butter and let the mixture warm for about 5 more minutes.

TIP: To amp up the protein, add 1 to 2 tablespoons of ground flaxseed or chia seeds.

HERBS AND SPICES: This recipe tastes great with warm spices like cinnamon and nutmeg.

BLUEBERRY-BANANA SMOOTHIE

• • •

YIELD: 4 SERVINGS   **PREP TIME:** 5 MINUTES

Smoothies are a great grab-and-go breakfast since they take only a few minutes to make and pour into a sippy cup or water bottle. I love adding greens to smoothies; baby spinach in particular takes on the flavor of any fruit it's paired with, making it a delicious and easy way to sneak some green veggies into your little one's diet.

GLUTEN-FREE

NUT-FREE

VG

VEGETARIAN

1 cup firmly packed baby spinach

1 cup fresh or frozen blueberries

½ cup fresh or frozen strawberries

1 banana

1 cup whole milk

1. In a high-powered blender, combine the spinach, blueberries, strawberries, banana, and milk. Blend until smooth.

2. Serve chilled. Store any remaining smoothie in the refrigerator for up to 24 hours.

TIP: Add 1 to 2 tablespoons of ground flaxseed or ground chia seeds to increase the protein in this smoothie. You can add ½ cup plain whole-milk Greek yogurt for more protein, as well.

SQUASH AND FRUIT PARFAIT

• • •

YIELD: 2 SERVINGS   **PREP TIME:** 5 MINUTES

A parfait is a decadent French dessert made with custard, cream, and layers of fruit. This healthy version is made with layers of plain whole-milk yogurt, fruit, and roasted butternut squash. The combination of apples or pears and butternut squash is perfect in the fall, and the yogurt gives it a creamy, tangy boost.

GLUTEN-FREE

NUT-FREE

VG

VEGETARIAN

1 cup plain whole-milk yogurt

1 cup cubed butternut squash, roasted or steamed

1 cup cubed apples or pears

2 pinches ground cinnamon

2 pinches ground nutmeg

1. In a small bowl, layer ¼ cup of yogurt, ½ cup of squash, another ¼ cup of yogurt, ½ cup of apples, 1 pinch of cinnamon, and 1 pinch of nutmeg (in that order). Repeat this process.

TIP: For a thicker parfait, use plain whole-milk Greek yogurt.

STORAGE: Store any leftovers in the refrigerator for up to 3 days.

VEGGIE OMELET WITH CHEESE

● ● ●

YIELD: 2 SERVINGS   **PREP TIME:** 10 MINUTES   **COOK TIME:** 15 MINUTES

Eggs are an excellent source of protein, healthy fats, and B vitamins, and the veggies add a hearty dose of fiber, making this a well-rounded morning meal that will keep your toddler full and satisfied. Enjoy this one together.

GLUTEN-FREE

NUT-FREE

VG
VEGETARIAN

2 teaspoons olive oil, divided

½ bell pepper (any color), seeded and diced

¼ red onion, diced

1 cup lightly packed shredded baby spinach

2 eggs

Pinch kosher salt

Pinch freshly ground black pepper

¼ cup shredded Cheddar cheese

1. In a large nonstick skillet over medium-high heat, heat 1 teaspoon of olive oil. Add the bell pepper, onion, and spinach. Cook for about 5 minutes, stirring frequently, until the veggies are soft. Transfer the vegetables to a small bowl.

2. In a medium bowl, beat the eggs with a fork or whisk until well blended. Add the salt and pepper.

3. Reheat the skillet over medium-high heat with the remaining 1 teaspoon of olive oil. Quickly pour the egg mixture into the skillet.

4. Using a rubber spatula, gently push the cooked edges of the eggs toward the center so that any uncooked eggs will contact the hot skillet's surface. Continue cooking, tilting the skillet and gently moving the eggs as needed.

5. When the top of the eggs has thickened and no visible liquid egg remains, place the veggie mixture onto one side of the omelet, and sprinkle the cheese over the vegetables. Using the spatula, fold the other side of the omelet over the vegetables. Gently slide the omelet onto a plate. Serve immediately.

TIP: Try adding fresh herbs like oregano, basil, or parsley.

DEALING WITH PICKY EATERS

Many toddlers between the ages of 12 and 18 months will start to exhibit signs of picky eating. This is completely normal from a developmental standpoint; it is their way of asserting control over one of the few things they have control over. That said, it's important not to give in to your little one's picky-eating tendencies, because that can set the stage for a *very* picky eater later on. Here are some tips for how to power through that stage and raise an adventurous eater.

Don't give in. Even if your child wants to eat only two or three things, continue to offer a variety of foods. One way to get children to try foods they might be rejecting is to alternate bites between foods they love and ones they don't. Eventually, they'll get used to the new food.

Be patient. It can take six months for a child to accept a food she's been rejecting. Toddlers sometimes need to try a food 30 to 40 times before they start to like it. Just continue to offer a wide variety of options, and your child will eventually come around.

Role-model for your child. Eat the foods you want them to eat. Have family dinners where everyone is eating the same foods. Resist the urge to make separate meals for your child—you're not a short-order cook! And encourage your child to try foods he is skeptical about; you can sweeten the deal by offering foods he likes as a reward.

Restrict treats for the first two years. Kids naturally love pizza, white and refined grains, and sweets. But if you raise your child on sprouted-wheat breads, whole-wheat pasta, vegetables, less-sweet fruits, beans, spices, herbs, and nuts early on, that's what she'll be used to, and she won't crave "kid foods" that populate most restaurant kid menus. There is plenty of time for children to enjoy treats after they turn two, but for that first year after purées (12 to 24 months), definitely place the focus on nutritious whole foods so you can raise a healthy, well-rounded, and adventurous eater.

AVOCADO TOAST

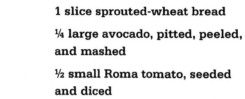

• • •

YIELD: 2 SERVINGS   **PREP TIME:** 5 MINUTES

My daughter absolutely loves avocado toast, and what's not to love? I like adding a bit of lemon juice to the avocado mixture to prevent it from browning. You can also sprinkle some shredded mild Cheddar cheese on top for a protein boost.

DAIRY-FREE

NUT-FREE

V

VEGAN

VG

VEGETARIAN

1 slice sprouted-wheat bread

¼ large avocado, pitted, peeled, and mashed

½ small Roma tomato, seeded and diced

¼ to ½ teaspoon freshly squeezed lemon juice

Pinch paprika

Pinch salt

1. Toast the bread until it's lightly browned but still soft.

2. In a small bowl, combine the avocado, tomato, lemon juice, paprika, and salt.

3. Spread the avocado mixture onto the toast and serve right away.

TIP: Avocado toast can be the base for many variations. Some fun ideas to top your avocado toast: grilled corn and crumbled feta cheese, pear and nut butter, garlic and goat cheese, pesto and lemon, and scrambled eggs.

12 TO 36 MONTHS

VEGGIE CHILI

• • •

YIELD: 8 SERVINGS   **PREP TIME:** 10 MINUTES   **COOK TIME:** 20 MINUTES

Hearty beans, crunchy veggies, and spices make this a surefire winner with your whole family. To make it work for everyone, try my strategy: I often separate out a portion for Layla before adding spices for the adults.

DAIRY-FREE

GLUTEN-FREE

NUT-FREE

(V)

VEGAN

VEGETARIAN

2 teaspoons olive oil

½ cup frozen corn kernels

2 red bell peppers, seeded and diced

½ red onion, diced

1 (15-ounce) can crushed tomatoes

1 (15-ounce) can kidney, black, or pinto beans

Salt

Freshly ground black pepper

1. Pour the olive oil into a large pot and heat over medium heat. Add the corn, bell peppers, and onion, and sauté until soft, about 5 minutes.

2. Add the crushed tomatoes with their juices, beans, and salt and pepper to taste. Simmer over medium heat for about 15 minutes or until cooked through.

TIP: Garnish with plain whole-milk Greek yogurt or shredded Cheddar cheese before serving.

STORAGE: Store any leftovers in the refrigerator for up to 3 days.

HERBS AND SPICES: To enhance the flavor for more mature palates, after portioning out a serving of the basic chili for your little one, add 1 minced garlic clove, ½ teaspoon ground cumin, ½ teaspoon ground coriander, ½ teaspoon smoked paprika, and ½ teaspoon regular paprika to the chili mixture.

FRENCH TOAST BREAD PUDDING

● ● ●

YIELD: 8 SERVINGS   **PREP TIME:** 10 MINUTES   **COOK TIME:** 45 MINUTES

French toast sounds indulgent, but it can actually be very healthy when you use sprouted-wheat bread and a sugarless batter. Consider making a big batch of this delicious bread pudding for the whole family or to reheat for meals later in the week.

NUT-FREE

(VG)

VEGETARIAN

Olive oil spray

8 slices sprouted-wheat bread, cut into 1-inch cubes

4 ounces cream cheese, at room temperature

1¼ cups unsweetened soy milk (I like WestSoy, with just two ingredients: organic soybeans and water)

1 cup egg whites or store-bought 100% liquid egg whites

1 tablespoon maple syrup

1 tablespoon butter

1. Preheat the oven to 350°F. Coat an 8-by-8-inch baking dish with olive oil spray. Spread the bread cubes evenly over the bottom of the dish.

2. In a blender, combine the cream cheese, soy milk, egg whites, maple syrup, and butter. Blend until smooth. Pour the mixture over the bread, making sure to soak it thoroughly.

3. Bake for about 45 minutes until the egg mixture is firm and cooked through. Let it cool slightly, then cut into 8 squares.

TIP: For extra flavor, add ¼ teaspoon ground cinnamon and ¼ teaspoon vanilla extract to the batter before pouring it over the bread. You can also sprinkle a handful of fresh fruit (berries, diced apples, peaches, or pears) on top of the bread cubes before pouring the egg mixture over it, or add some banana slices at serving time.

STORAGE: This will keep in the refrigerator for up to 3 days.

CORN, ZUCCHINI, AND SPINACH FLATBREAD

• • •

YIELD: 4 SERVINGS   **PREP TIME:** 10 MINUTES   **COOK TIME:** 15 MINUTES

Fresh corn, summer squash, and greens make a delicate and summery topping for this crowd-pleasing flatbread. Here I use naan, but you can use any type of base you like: Whole-wheat pita bread, sprouted-wheat English muffins, and even sprouted-wheat tortillas can all work just as well.

NUT-FREE

VG

VEGETARIAN

1 teaspoon olive oil

½ zucchini, quartered and sliced

½ cup fresh or frozen corn kernels

1 cup shredded baby spinach

1 piece whole-wheat naan bread

¼ cup shredded mozzarella or Parmesan cheese

1. Preheat the oven to 350°F.

2. In a large skillet, heat the olive oil over medium heat. Add the zucchini, corn, and spinach, and cook until soft, 5 to 10 minutes.

3. Toast the naan bread lightly and place on a small baking sheet. Top with the veggie mixture and the cheese. Bake for 5 minutes or until the cheese has melted.

4. Cut into 4 pieces and serve warm.

HERBS AND SPICES: To make this dish even more flavorful, add 1 teaspoon fresh thyme leaves and 1 minced garlic clove with the veggies.

VEGGIE QUESADILLAS

• • •

YIELD: 2 SERVINGS   **PREP TIME:** 10 MINUTES   **COOK TIME:** 10 MINUTES

I haven't met a child who doesn't like quesadillas. By using a wheat tortilla, fresh veggies, and refried black beans, you can create a healthy twist on this beloved classic without losing any of the flavor of the original recipe. And yes, you get to keep the cheese.

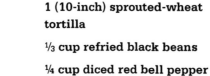

NUT-FREE

VEGETARIAN

1 (10-inch) sprouted-wheat tortilla

⅓ cup refried black beans

¼ cup diced red bell pepper

¼ cup diced tomatoes

¼ cup shredded Cheddar cheese

Olive oil spray

1. Lay the tortilla on a flat surface. Spread the black beans over half the tortilla, top the black beans with the bell pepper and tomatoes, and sprinkle with the cheese. Fold the other half of the tortilla over the filling.

2. Heat a small skillet over medium heat and coat it with olive oil spray.

3. Place the quesadilla in the skillet. Cook over medium-low heat for 5 minutes or until the cheese has begun to melt. Carefully flip and cook for another 5 minutes, until slightly brown and crispy. Cut into halves or quarters and serve.

TIP: If your little one is getting fussy about eating veggies, these quesadillas are a great vehicle to "sneak" extra veggies into his diet. One of my favorite tricks is to chop up baby spinach super fine, sauté it, and mix it into the refried beans. Your little one won't be able to recognize it, but he will get a healthy serving of greens in his meal!

RED LENTIL DAL WITH SPINACH

• • •

YIELD: 8 SERVINGS **PREP TIME:** 20 MINUTES **COOK TIME:** 25 MINUTES

Dal is an Indian dish that's made by simmering split peas or lentils until they have melted into a flavorful stew. This particular version contains spinach for additional fiber, iron, and B vitamins. Consider making a double batch and stowing some in the freezer for those nights when you don't have time to cook.

FREEZER-FRIENDLY

DAIRY-FREE

GLUTEN-FREE

NUT-FREE

V

VEGAN

VG

VEGETARIAN

1 teaspoon olive oil

⅓ cup chopped onion

⅓ cup chopped celery

⅓ cup chopped carrot

1 cup dried red lentils, rinsed and picked over

1 cup water

1 (15-ounce) can crushed tomatoes

4 cups chopped baby spinach

1 cup light coconut milk

Salt

1. Heat a large soup pot over medium-high heat. Add the olive oil, onion, celery, and carrot, and cook for about 5 minutes until the vegetables are fragrant and translucent. Add spices (if using).

2. Add the lentils, water, tomatoes with their juices, spinach, and coconut milk.

3. Bring to a boil, then reduce the heat to a low simmer. Cook, covered, for about 20 minutes, stirring occasionally, until the lentils are soft. If the liquid evaporates before the lentils are done cooking, just add a little bit more water and continue to cook.

4. Season to taste with salt and serve.

TIP: Serve this stew with brown rice or quinoa to make it even more filling and delicious.

HERBS AND SPICES: To add more flavor to this recipe, I recommend adding 3 minced garlic cloves, 1 teaspoon grated ginger, 1 teaspoon mild curry powder, 1 teaspoon ground coriander, and ½ teaspoon garam masala.

NUT BUTTER PINWHEELS

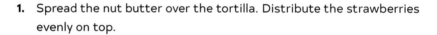

YIELD: 2 SERVINGS   **PREP TIME:** 10 MINUTES

I don't make traditional peanut-butter-and-jelly sandwiches because of the high sugar content in most jams and jellies. Instead, I use chopped fruit or fruit purées. This version uses strawberries, but feel free to use any fruit you like. Pears, apples, blueberries, and bananas all work well, and you really will come to prefer them over sugary jams.

DAIRY-FREE

(V)

VEGAN

(VG)

VEGETARIAN

2 tablespoons nut butter (almond butter and peanut butter work well)

1 (10-inch) sprouted-wheat tortilla

1 cup strawberries, finely chopped in a food processor or blender

1. Spread the nut butter over the tortilla. Distribute the strawberries evenly on top.

2. Roll the tortilla into a log.

3. Cut into 1-inch pieces and serve.

TIP: You can make savory pinwheels by using cream cheese and veggies instead of nut butter and fruit.

12 TO 36 MONTHS

CUCUMBER-HUMMUS WRAP

• • •

YIELD: 2 SERVINGS   **PREP TIME:** 10 MINUTES

Wraps are a breeze to make, and the combination of the sprouted-wheat tortilla, cheese, and hummus makes this a protein-filled, vegetarian-friendly meal that your little one is sure to love.

DAIRY-FREE

NUT-FREE

(V)
VEGAN

(VG)
VEGETARIAN

2 tablespoons hummus

1 (10-inch) sprouted-wheat tortilla

¼ cup baby spinach

½ cucumber, diced

1 small tomato, diced

1. Spread the hummus over the tortilla. Add the spinach, cucumber, and tomato evenly on top.

2. Roll the tortilla into a log.

3. Cut into 1-inch pieces and serve.

TIP: Add ⅛ cup shredded cheese for some added protein. Your wrap will still be vegetarian this way, though not vegan or dairy-free. Once your baby gets older and can hold sandwiches better, you can take these ingredients and pop them in a whole-wheat pita or between two slices of sprouted wheat bread for a healthy and filling sandwich.

PEANUT NOODLES WITH BROCCOLI AND TOFU

• • •

YIELD: 8 SERVINGS   **PREP TIME:** 10 MINUTES   **COOK TIME:** 15 MINUTES

My daughter loves noodles and will eat just about anything when it's paired with a noodle. Instead of refined, white-flour noodles, I use whole-wheat spaghetti, which adds a pleasant nutty flavor to this flavorful Asian-inspired dish.

DAIRY-FREE

VEGAN

VEGETARIAN

4 ounces whole-wheat spaghetti

1 teaspoon olive oil

8 ounces firm tofu, cut into ½-inch cubes

1 cup broccoli florets, steamed and cut into small pieces

⅓ cup creamy peanut butter

4 tablespoons coconut milk

1. Cook the spaghetti according to package directions. Drain and set aside.

2. Pour the olive oil into a medium skillet and heat over medium heat. Add the tofu and broccoli, and sauté for about 5 minutes, then add the spaghetti and mix, warming gently.

3. In a blender, or in a medium bowl using a whisk, blend the peanut butter and coconut milk until smooth. Add the spice (if using).

4. Add the peanut butter sauce to the spaghetti mixture. Serve warm.

TIP: To add even more veggies into your baby's diet, try zucchini noodles or sweet potato noodles in place of the spaghetti.

HERBS AND SPICES: Try adding 2 teaspoons mild curry powder to the peanut butter sauce before adding it to the spaghetti—it tastes great.

PITA PIZZA

• • •

YIELD: 2 SERVINGS **PREP TIME:** 10 MINUTES **COOK TIME:** 15 MINUTES

Friday night is pizza night in our house, and I love setting up a "pizza assembly station" with all of the toppings laid out. That way, my daughter can create her own pizza with the toppings of her choice. We always use whole-wheat pita bread to make individual-size, healthier pizzas and include several veggie options for toppings. For a Mexican-inspired pizza, try substituting refried black beans for pizza sauce and a Mexican shredded cheese blend instead of Parmesan or mozzarella.

NUT-FREE

VG

VEGETARIAN

1 teaspoon olive oil

1 cup shredded baby spinach

1 tomato, diced

½ red bell pepper, seeded and diced

1 large whole-wheat pita bread

½ cup homemade or canned pizza sauce

¼ cup shredded Parmesan or mozzarella cheese

1. Preheat the oven to 350°F.

2. Heat the olive oil in a medium skillet over medium heat. Add the spinach, tomato, and bell pepper. Cook until soft, about 5 minutes.

3. Toast the pita bread lightly and place it on a medium baking sheet.

4. Top the pita bread with the pizza sauce, then the veggie mixture, and then the cheese. Bake in the oven for 5 to 10 minutes, until the cheese has melted and the pita bread is slightly crispy.

5. Cut into 4 pieces and serve warm.

TIP: Fresh herbs taste great in this recipe. I like adding fresh basil, garlic, and oregano to the veggie mixture as it cooks. One teaspoon of dried Italian seasoning is also tasty.

RICE AND BEANS

• • •

YIELD: 8 SERVINGS **PREP TIME:** 10 MINUTES **COOK TIME:** 10 MINUTES

Rice and beans is one of the heartiest vegetarian dishes you can make, since the rice and beans together form a complete protein. You can add any cooked veggies you like to this dish. We often dress this up with a topping or two (see Tip).

DAIRY-FREE

GLUTEN-FREE

NUT-FREE

(V)

VEGAN

(VG)

VEGETARIAN

2 teaspoons olive oil

½ red onion, finely chopped

1 red bell pepper, seeded and finely chopped

1 (15-ounce) can black beans, rinsed and drained

1 cup cooked brown rice or quinoa

½ cup fresh or canned crushed tomatoes

1. In a medium skillet, heat the olive oil over medium heat. Add the red onion, red bell pepper, and black beans. Sauté for 5 minutes, until soft.

2. Add the rice and crushed tomatoes with their juices. Cook until warm, about 5 minutes, and serve.

TIP: Add 1 teaspoon ground cumin, 1 teaspoon ground coriander, ½ teaspoon mild chili powder, and 2 minced garlic cloves in step 1 to add even more flavor to this recipe. You can also add baby spinach, diced cooked butternut squash, or sweet potatoes to add more fiber. Topping this dish with avocado, shredded Cheddar cheese, or plain whole-milk Greek yogurt is another great way to add more nutrition and protein.

BUTTERNUT SQUASH AND CHICKPEA TAGINE

• • •

YIELD: 8 SERVINGS **PREP TIME:** 10 MINUTES **COOK TIME:** 30 MINUTES

A tagine is a Moroccan dish named after the earthenware pot in which it's cooked. Warm spices, nuts, stewed vegetables, and legumes are characteristic of this dish, though in many cases it includes slow-cooked meats as well. This vegetarian variation delivers a cozy, comforting meal on a cold night.

DAIRY-FREE

GLUTEN-FREE

NUT-FREE

(V)

VEGAN

(VG)

VEGETARIAN

1 teaspoon olive oil

½ red onion, diced

3 zucchini, diced

1 (16-ounce) package frozen butternut squash, thawed

1 (15-ounce) can chickpeas, rinsed and drained

1 (15-ounce) can diced fire-roasted tomatoes

¼ cup diced dried apricots

½ cup low-sodium vegetable broth

Salt

1 tablespoon smooth almond butter

1. In a large pot over medium heat, heat the olive oil. Sauté the onion, zucchini, and butternut squash until soft, 5 to 10 minutes.

2. Add the chickpeas, tomatoes with their juices, apricots, and broth. Season with salt to taste. Lower the heat to medium-low and cook for about 20 minutes.

3. Remove about ½ cup of the cooking liquid and pour it into a small bowl. Add the almond butter and whisk until smooth, then pour this back into the tagine. Stir to incorporate, and serve.

TIP: This tagine tastes great over brown rice or quinoa, or with plain whole-milk yogurt. To amp up the flavor even more, try adding 3 minced garlic cloves, 1 teaspoon mild curry powder, 1 teaspoon ground cumin, and a sprinkle of cinnamon to the veggies before adding the chickpeas and other ingredients.

BLACK BEAN BURRITO BOWL

• • •

YIELD: 8 SERVINGS   **PREP TIME:** 10 MINUTES   **COOK TIME:** 20 MINUTES

While I love burritos, they aren't a great option for little hands since the filling all falls out while your toddler is trying to eat it. Enter the burrito bowl, which contains all of the tasty ingredients of a burrito in a form that your toddler can consume with ease.

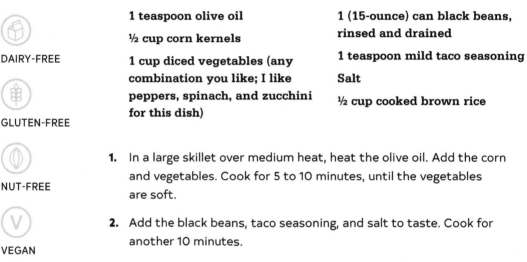

DAIRY-FREE

GLUTEN-FREE

NUT-FREE

V
VEGAN

VG
VEGETARIAN

1 teaspoon olive oil

½ cup corn kernels

1 cup diced vegetables (any combination you like; I like peppers, spinach, and zucchini for this dish)

1 (15-ounce) can black beans, rinsed and drained

1 teaspoon mild taco seasoning

Salt

½ cup cooked brown rice

1. In a large skillet over medium heat, heat the olive oil. Add the corn and vegetables. Cook for 5 to 10 minutes, until the vegetables are soft.

2. Add the black beans, taco seasoning, and salt to taste. Cook for another 10 minutes.

3. Warm the brown rice and serve it with the black bean mixture.

TIP: As your little one gets older, try additional toppings for this burrito bowl, like cottage cheese or plain whole-milk Greek yogurt, shredded Cheddar cheese, minced red onion, diced tomatoes, and shredded lettuce.

VEGGIE STIR-FRY

● ● ●

YIELD: 8 SERVINGS   **PREP TIME:** 10 MINUTES   **COOK TIME:** 20 MINUTES

My daughter will eat just about any vegetable if it has soy sauce on it. This stir-fry, made with protein-rich tofu and a variety of vegetables, is a nutritional superstar and a surefire hit with little ones. Use frozen mixed vegetables to save on prep time.

DAIRY-FREE

GLUTEN-FREE

VEGAN

VG

VEGETARIAN

1 teaspoon olive oil

1 (16-ounce) package frozen mixed vegetables (like broccoli, green beans, and carrots)

3 garlic cloves, minced

8 ounces firm tofu, cut into ½-inch cubes

2 teaspoons low-sodium soy sauce

1 tablespoon peanut butter

1. In a large skillet over medium heat, heat the olive oil. Add the frozen mixed vegetables and cook through, stirring, until soft, about 10 minutes.

2. Add the garlic, tofu, soy sauce, and peanut butter. Stir to combine, and cook for 10 minutes more.

3. Adjust the seasoning, adding more soy sauce if desired.

TIP: Try serving this stir-fry with brown rice or quinoa for some added whole grains.

HERBS AND SPICES: Add 1 teaspoon minced ginger to this dish for a more complex flavor.

12 TO 36 MONTHS

PENNE WITH SPINACH PESTO

...

YIELD: 8 SERVINGS   **PREP TIME:** 10 MINUTES

Traditional pesto is made with basil. This version gets a nutritious, leafy-green boost by using spinach as well. Paired with whole-wheat penne and topped with cheese, this variation on the classic is a guaranteed winner.

DAIRY-FREE

VG

VEGETARIAN

6 ounces baby spinach

¼ cup slivered blanched almonds

¼ cup lightly packed fresh basil

2 large garlic cloves, chopped

2 tablespoons vegetable broth

2 teaspoons freshly squeezed lemon juice

¼ teaspoon salt

1 tablespoon olive oil

1 cup cooked whole-wheat penne

1. In a blender, combine the spinach, almonds, basil, and garlic. Pulse to blend.

2. Add the broth, lemon juice, salt, and olive oil. Purée until combined.

3. In a medium bowl, toss the pesto with the cooked penne (reheat the pasta first, if necessary). Serve warm.

TIP: This pasta tastes great with cooked fresh vegetables tossed in at the end, too. Some of my favorites are tomatoes and summer squash.

HERBS AND SPICES: For even more flavor, add 2 teaspoons fresh oregano, 1 teaspoon fresh thyme, ¼ teaspoon freshly ground black pepper, and ¼ cup shredded Parmesan cheese along with the broth and other ingredients before puréeing.

DINING OUT

Now that your little one is old enough to sit at the table, you might begin having some fun eating out as a family. Restaurant dining with a toddler can be unpredictable, but there are a few things you can do to ensure a greater chance of success. Here are some of my favorite, tried-and-true tips for dining out with a toddler in tow:

Choose family-friendly restaurants at first. Look for an establishment that's frequented by families with children. These are likely to have high chairs and crayons for your child to draw with while waiting for the food to arrive, as well as a noisier atmosphere in which to blend in!

Plan dinner around nap times. The worst experience we had with Layla was when we took her out for dinner when she was clearly tired and ready for bed. A well-rested child is a happy child. If that means eating lunch at 2 p.m. after your toddler's nap, or going out for dinner at 5 p.m. before your toddler's bedtime, it's well worth it, for everyone's enjoyment.

Bring a bag of tricks. I always bring a small bag of toys and games for my daughter to keep her entertained while waiting for her food. Small toys that fit on a high chair, crayons and paper, and finger puppets are all great for keeping a toddler occupied.

Don't expect to settle in for a leisurely meal. Toddlers have short attention spans, so spending more than 30 to 45 minutes in a high chair might be unrealistic. Before you get to the restaurant, look at the menu online so you can place your order when you sit down. Order drinks and meals at once, perhaps skipping the appetizer the first few times. When your food arrives, ask for the check so that you can make a swift exit when you're done eating.

Engage your child. Any amount of grown-up conversation might be too much to expect at first. Your toddler will enjoy the dining experience more if you spend time chatting and engaging with her, making her feel like a guest of honor. Over time, dining out will become more routine and you'll probably get to start sneaking in some conversations of your own.

TURKEY FRIED RICE

• • •

YIELD: 8 (¼-CUP) SERVINGS   **PREP TIME:** 10 MINUTES   **COOK TIME:** 20 MINUTES

The entire family is sure to enjoy this tasty classic, and it's a snap to make when you use precooked brown rice. Cook the rice according to package instructions and then, if you like, freeze it in zip-top bags for up to 3 months.

FREEZER-FRIENDLY

DAIRY-FREE

GLUTEN-FREE

NUT-FREE

2 tablespoons olive oil

6 ounces ground turkey

3 scallions, finely chopped

½ teaspoon grated fresh ginger

1 cup frozen peas

1 garlic clove, minced

1 egg, beaten

1½ cups cooked brown rice

1 tablespoon soy sauce or gluten-free soy sauce

1. In a large skillet over medium-high heat, heat the olive oil until it shimmers.

2. Add the turkey and cook, crumbling with a spoon, until browned, 5 to 7 minutes.

3. Add the scallions, ginger, peas, and garlic. Cook, stirring occasionally, for 4 minutes more.

4. Add the egg and cook, stirring constantly, until the egg is set, about 3 minutes.

5. Add the rice and soy sauce. Cook to heat through, 2 to 3 minutes more.

TIP: You can make this vegan by omitting the meat and egg altogether and instead adding 6 ounces tofu cut into ¼-inch pieces.

STORAGE: Refrigerate for up to 3 days. Freeze for up to 3 months in single-serving containers.

EASY COD CAKES

• • •

YIELD: 12 CAKES   **PREP TIME:** 10 MINUTES   **COOK TIME:** 20 TO 25 MINUTES

Cod cakes are a nice alternative to chicken nuggets, and your little one will enjoy dipping them in this healthy and tangy sauce that takes only seconds to make. If you can't get your hands on cod, any whitefish will do the trick.

FREEZER-FRIENDLY

NUT-FREE

FOR THE COD CAKES

6 ounces cod or other whitefish, bones and skin removed

Pinch sea salt plus ½ teaspoon, used later

1 egg, beaten

¼ cup bread crumbs (regular or gluten-free)

½ teaspoon garlic powder

½ teaspoon dried dill

FOR THE SAUCE

¼ cup plain yogurt

2 tablespoons chopped fresh dill

1 tablespoon freshly squeezed lemon juice

¼ teaspoon sea salt

1. Preheat the oven to 350°F. Line a medium rimmed baking sheet with parchment paper.

2. Place the cod in a small skillet, and add the pinch of salt and enough water to cover the fish. Simmer until the cod is opaque and fully cooked, about 5 minutes (depending on the thickness of the fish). Transfer the cod to a plate and allow it to cool, then flake it into very small pieces.

3. In a medium bowl, combine the flaked cod, egg, bread crumbs, garlic powder, dill, and the remaining ½ teaspoon of salt.

4. Form the cod mixture into 12 small balls and flatten them. Place them on the prepared baking sheet.

5. Bake until golden, 15 to 20 minutes.

TO MAKE THE SAUCE

In a small bowl, whisk together the yogurt, dill, lemon juice, and salt, and serve on the side for dipping.

TIP: You can make the cod cakes ahead for easy mealtime preparation. Roll the balls, flatten them, and put them on a plate. Cover tightly and refrigerate until needed. (Add a few minutes to the baking time if you're doing this.)

STORAGE: Refrigerate for up to 3 days. Freeze for up to 3 months in a zip-top bag.

CHICKEN NOODLE SOUP

• • •

YIELD: 6 SERVINGS **PREP TIME:** 10 MINUTES **COOK TIME:** 15 MINUTES

This soup freezes very well, so you can make big batches and keep it for those busy days when you don't have time to cook from scratch—or when someone little (or big) gets the sniffles. It's a delicious and satisfying alternative to canned chicken soup, which tends to be high in sodium and preservatives.

FREEZER-
FRIENDLY

DAIRY-FREE

NUT-FREE

2 tablespoons olive oil

½ onion, finely chopped

1 carrot, peeled and cut into
¼-inch cubes

1 celery stalk, cut into
¼-inch cubes

1 garlic clove, minced

6 cups low-sodium or unsalted
chicken broth

½ teaspoon salt (optional
if using unsalted broth)

1 teaspoon dried thyme

8 ounces boneless, skinless
chicken breasts, cut into
¼-inch cubes

4 ounces bite-size
whole-wheat noodles

1. In a large pot, heat the olive oil over medium-high heat until it shimmers.

2. Add the onion, carrot, and celery and cook, stirring occasionally, until the vegetables are soft, about 5 minutes.

3. Add the garlic and cook, stirring constantly, for 30 seconds.

4. Add the chicken broth, salt (if using), thyme, cubed chicken, and noodles. Lower the heat to medium and simmer until the chicken is cooked through and the noodles are soft, about 10 minutes.

TIP: To make this gluten-free, choose gluten-free noodles or make the noodles from zucchini. You may be able to buy precut zucchini noodles in the produce section of your grocery store. If you use zucchini noodles, add them in the last 5 minutes of cooking.

STORAGE: Refrigerate for up to 3 days. Freeze for up to 4 months.

12 TO 36 MONTHS

SPAGHETTI WITH MEAT SAUCE

• • •

YIELD: 4 SERVINGS   **PREP TIME:** 5 MINUTES   **COOK TIME:** 20 MINUTES

This simple, classic comfort-food recipe is sure to appeal to all ages. Chopping the spaghetti up into shorter pieces before you cook it makes perfect bite-size pasta for your little one.

FREEZER
FRIENDLY

DAIRY-FREE

NUT-FREE

1 tablespoon olive oil

8 ounces lean ground beef

¼ cup finely chopped onion

1 garlic clove, minced

2 cups canned crushed tomatoes, drained

½ teaspoon dried oregano

4 ounces dried whole-wheat spaghetti, broken into pieces

1. In a medium nonstick skillet over medium-high heat, heat the olive oil until it shimmers.

2. Add the ground beef and cook, crumbling and stirring, until browned, 5 to 7 minutes.

3. Add the onion and cook until it is soft, 3 to 5 minutes more.

4. Add the garlic and cook, stirring constantly, for 30 seconds.

5. Add the crushed tomatoes and oregano. Bring to a simmer and cook, stirring occasionally, for about 5 minutes.

6. Meanwhile, cook the spaghetti according to the package directions and drain well.

7. Add the cooked spaghetti to the sauce and toss to combine.

TIP: Other pasta shapes will work with the sauce, as well, such as orzo or rotini. To make this dish vegan, replace the ground beef with 1 cup of cooked lentils.

STORAGE: Refrigerate for up to 3 days. Freeze the pasta separately from the sauce for best results. Freeze for up to 3 months.

SWEET POTATO AND GROUND LAMB SHEPHERD'S PIE

• • •

YIELD: 6 SERVINGS   **PREP TIME:** 15 MINUTES   **COOK TIME:** 55 MINUTES

Double this recipe and it suddenly becomes an easy and tasty meal for the whole family. Although it does involve several steps and different dishes to cook it, the result is a hearty and nourishing meal everyone is sure to love. Since it freezes well, why not stash some away in single-serving containers for last-minute meals?

FREEZER-FRIENDLY

DAIRY-FREE

GLUTEN-FREE

NUT-FREE

1½ medium sweet potatoes, peeled and cut into ½-inch cubes

¼ cup milk (dairy or non-dairy)

2 tablespoons olive oil

8 ounces ground lamb

½ onion, finely chopped

1 cup diced fresh or frozen carrots

1 cup fresh or frozen peas

1 teaspoon dried thyme

½ teaspoon sea salt

⅛ teaspoon freshly ground black pepper

½ teaspoon garlic powder

3 cups unsalted chicken broth

1 tablespoon cornstarch

1. Preheat the oven to 400°F.

2. In a large saucepan, cover the sweet potatoes with water and simmer, covered, until soft, about 10 minutes.

3. Drain the potatoes and transfer them to a medium bowl. Mash them with the milk. Set aside.

4. In a large skillet over medium-high heat, heat the olive oil until it shimmers.

5. Add the ground lamb and cook, crumbling and stirring, until browned, 5 to 7 minutes.

6. Add the onion and cook until it is soft, 3 to 5 minutes more.

7. Add the carrots, peas, thyme, salt, pepper, and garlic powder.

8. In a small bowl, whisk the chicken broth and cornstarch. Add this liquid to the pot. Cook, stirring constantly, until the liquid thickens, about 3 minutes.

9. Spread the mixture in a 9-by-9-inch baking pan, patting and leveling to make a smooth surface. Spread the mashed sweet potatoes over the top.

10. Bake until bubbly, about 30 minutes.

TIP: You can replace the carrots and peas with any vegetables you wish; mixed frozen veggies work well (up to 2 cups). You can also replace the ground lamb with 1½ cups cooked lentils—or a combination of lentils and rice—to make this vegan.

STORAGE: Refrigerate for up to 3 days. Freeze for up to 4 months in single-serving portions.

BEEF AND BARLEY STEW

• • •

YIELD: 6 SERVINGS   **PREP TIME:** 10 MINUTES   **COOK TIME:** 20 MINUTES

Pearl barley is a fun grain for kids because the grains are small in size and add a satisfying texture to foods. Pearl barley has had the bran and germ polished away, so it isn't a whole grain, but it's still a good source of fiber, manganese, selenium, and magnesium. Since pearl barley takes about 40 minutes to cook, you might want to cook up a big batch and freeze it in 1-cup servings so it's easy to have ready on weeknights.

FREEZER-FRIENDLY

DAIRY-FREE

NUT-FREE

2 tablespoons olive oil

8 ounces lean ground beef

¼ cup finely chopped onion

1 carrot, peeled and chopped

2 tablespoons all-purpose flour

3 cups unsalted chicken broth

1 cup frozen peas

¾ teaspoon dried thyme

½ teaspoon garlic powder

½ teaspoon sea salt

1½ cups cooked pearl barley

1. In a large pot over medium-high heat, heat the olive oil until it shimmers.

2. Add the ground beef and cook, stirring, until browned, 5 to 7 minutes.

3. Add the onion and carrot and cook until they are soft, 3 to 5 minutes more.

4. Add the flour and cook, stirring constantly, for 1 minute.

5. Add the chicken broth, peas, thyme, garlic powder, and salt. Cook, stirring occasionally, until the sauce thickens, about 4 minutes.

6. Stir in the cooked barley and heat through.

TIP: To make this gluten-free, replace the barley with rice and omit the flour. In place of the flour, whisk 1 tablespoon cornstarch into the chicken broth before adding it to the pot. To make this vegan, replace the ground beef with 1 pound cooked black beans or lentils.

STORAGE: Refrigerate for up to 3 days, or freeze for up to 4 months.

MINI GROUND BEEF AND VEGGIE MEATBALLS

• • •

YIELD: ABOUT 12 MEATBALLS   **PREP TIME:** 15 MINUTES   **COOK TIME:** 20 MINUTES

Many parents worry that meatballs are a choking hazard; however, they can be a safe and nutritious meal as long as you cut them into smaller, baby bite-size chunks before serving them to your toddler.

FREEZER-FRIENDLY

DAIRY-FREE

GLUTEN-FREE

NUT-FREE

6 ounces lean ground beef

½ teaspoon Dijon mustard

1 carrot, peeled and grated, water wrung out (see Tip)

1 zucchini, grated, water wrung out

½ onion, grated, water wrung out

½ teaspoon sea salt

½ teaspoon garlic powder

1 teaspoon gluten-free or regular soy sauce

1 egg, beaten

1. Preheat the oven to 400°F.

2. In a large bowl, combine the ground beef, mustard, carrot, zucchini, onion, salt, garlic powder, soy sauce, and egg.

3. Roll the mixture into ¾-inch meatballs and place on a medium rimmed baking sheet.

4. Bake until the meat is thoroughly cooked (with an internal temperature of 165°F), 16 to 18 minutes. Break several meatballs open to make sure there is no pink remaining.

TIP: To wring the water out of the vegetables, roll them up in a tea towel and squeeze over the sink until you've extracted as much water as possible.

STORAGE: Refrigerate for up to 3 days. Freeze for up to 4 months in zip-top bags.

MEASUREMENT CONVERSIONS

VOLUME EQUIVALENTS (LIQUID)

US STANDARD (OUNCES)	US STANDARD (APPROXIMATE)	METRIC
2 tablespoons	1 fl. oz.	30 mL
¼ cup	2 fl. oz.	60 mL
½ cup	4 fl. oz.	120 mL
1 cup	8 fl. oz.	240 mL
1½ cups	12 fl. oz.	355 mL
2 cups or 1 pint	16 fl. oz.	475 mL
4 cups or 1 quart	32 fl. oz.	1 L
1 gallon	128 fl. oz.	4 L

OVEN TEMPERATURES

FAHRENHEIT (F)	CELSIUS (C) (APPROXIMATE)
250°F	120°C
300°F	150°C
325°F	165°C
350°F	180°C
375°F	190°C
400°F	200°C
425°F	220°C
450°F	230°C

VOLUME EQUIVALENTS (DRY)

US STANDARD	METRIC (APPROXIMATE)
⅛ teaspoon	0.5 mL
¼ teaspoon	1 mL
½ teaspoon	2 mL
¾ teaspoon	4 mL
1 teaspoon	5 mL
1 tablespoon	15 mL
¼ cup	59 mL
⅓ cup	79 mL
½ cup	118 mL
⅔ cup	156 mL
¾ cup	177 mL
1 cup	235 mL
2 cups or 1 pint	475 mL
3 cups	700 mL
4 cups or 1 quart	1 L

WEIGHT EQUIVALENTS

US STANDARD	METRIC (APPROXIMATE)
½ ounce	15 g
1 ounce	30 g
2 ounces	60 g
4 ounces	115 g
8 ounces	225 g
12 ounces	340 g
16 ounces or 1 pound	455 g

REFERENCES

American Academy of Pediatrics. "Infant Food and Feeding." Accessed November 15, 2017. www.aap.org/en-us/advocacy-and-policy/aap-health-initiatives/HALF-Implementation -Guide/Age-Specific-Content/pages/infant-food-and-feeding.aspx.

Baranski, Marcin, Dominika Srednicka-Tober, Nikolaos Volakakis, Chris Seal, Roy Sanderson, Gavin B. Stewart, Charles Benbrook, et al. "Higher Antioxidant and Lower Cadmium Concentrations and Lower Incidence of Pesticide Residues in Organically Grown Crops: A Systematic Literature Review and Meta-analyses." *British Journal of Nutrition* 112, no. 5 (September 2014): 794–811. https://www.foodpolitics.com/wp-content/uploads /14-06-12-Final -Crops-Paper-BJN5552.pdf.

Environmental Working Group. "EWG's 2017 Shopper's Guide to Pesticides in Produce™." Accessed November 15, 2017. https://www.ewg.org/foodnews/summary.php# .Wma0zzOpkWo.

The Mayo Clinic. "Food Allergy vs. Food Intolerance: What's the Difference?" Accessed December 19, 2017. www.mayoclinic.org/diseases-conditions /food-allergyexpert-answers /food-allergy/faq-20058538.

US Food and Drug Administration. "Food Allergies: What You Need to Know." Accessed December 28, 2017. www.fda.gov/Food/ResourcesForYou/Consumers/ucm079311.htm.

RECIPE INDEX

INDEX

ACKNOWLEDGMENTS

Thank you to my husband Niral for being a great partner, my biggest cheerleader, and my best friend through this entire journey. Thank you for encouraging me to follow my dreams and for pushing me to experiment in the kitchen even when I wasn't confident I could create anything edible for us to eat! To my daughter, Layla—thank you for being my little taste tester—you are the most adventurous and curious eater, and so much fun to cook with! Watching you grow and learn has been a joy. To my son, Ayan—you have just arrived in this world and already are so observant and inquisitive. I can't wait for you to start eating solids —oh, the fun we will have! I couldn't be luckier to have all of you in my life.

To all of my readers of *The Picky Eater*: Thank you for sharing your experiences in healthy cooking with me, and for making what I do so rewarding. Your e-mails, comments, and messages about how my blog has helped you means the world to me!

Thank you to the entire Callisto Media team. My amazing editor, Meg Ilasco, you made it easy for this first-time author to embark on what could have seemed like an overwhelming project! You were a wonderful collaborator; flexible and supportive of my philosophy and approach. Thank you to Christina Henry de Tessan, Erum Khan, Hane Lee, and the editing team. And to Karen Frazier, our chef who helped with the meat recipes you see in this book.

To all of my dear friends, thank you for being there for me, laughing with me, commis-erating about our kids and experiences as parents together and lending a listening ear whenever I've needed it.

And of course, to my family: Dad (Baba), my late mom (Mommy), and Nikhil. I bet you never thought the girl who didn't know how to use a can opener would build a career and life around food! Thank you for always supporting me no matter what path I've chosen, and for raising me to love and appreciate healthy, wholesome, flavorful food.

ABOUT THE AUTHOR

ANJALI SHAH is a food writer, board-certified health coach, mom of two, and owner of *The Picky Eater*, a healthy-food-and-lifestyle blog. Her work has been featured in *Oprah.com*, *Women's Health*, *Cooking Light*, *Reader's Digest*, CNN, *BuzzFeed*, Food Network, *Glamour*, *Ladies' Home Journal*, Whole Foods, and *SHAPE*, and at Kaiser Permanente. Anjali grew up a "whole wheat" girl, but married a "white bread" kind of guy. Hoping to prove that nutritious food could in fact be delicious and desirable, she taught herself how to cook and successfully transformed her husband's eating habits from a diet of frozen pizzas and Taco Bell to her healthy yet flavorful recipes made with simple, wholesome ingredients. Through her blog, *The Picky Eater*, Anjali shares her passion for tasty, healthy cooking. When she isn't working with clients or media outlets, Anjali can be found playing with her four-year-old daughter, Layla, and infant, Ayan; spending time with her husband, Niral; or testing out new, healthy, family-friendly recipes for her blog.

FOLLOW OR CONNECT WITH ANJALI ONLINE:

www.pickyeaterblog.com
facebook.com/thepickyeater
twitter.com/pickyeaterblog
instagram.com/thepickyeater
pinterest.com/thepickyeater

CPSIA information can be obtained
at www.ICGtesting.com
Printed in the USA
BVOW11s1457080318
509519BV00001B/1/P